Carol A. Jones

Substitute Teacher's Reference Manual

FOURTH EDITION

ETC Publications
Palm Springs, California

Library of Congress Cataloging-in-Publication Data

Jones, Carol A., 1952-
   The substitute teacher's reference manual / by Carol A. Jones.--4th ed.
      p.cm
   ISBN 0-88280-150-3
   1. Substitute teachers--Handbooks, manuals, etc. I. Title

   LB2844.1.S8J65 2001
   371.14'122--dc21

                                              00-069126

★★★

Published by ETC Publications
   Palm Springs
   California 92262

Published in the United States of America.

CONTENTS

Introduction

When I worked as a substitute teacher, I often found it frustrating that there were few if any resources available for me to use in the classroom. As a Language Arts teacher, who sometimes needs to procure a substitute teacher for my classroom, I often find myself writing endless notes to the substitute teacher, to insure that both the teacher and the students have a successful day. It was for these reasons that I wrote the first edition of the book, *Substitute Teacher's Reference Manual*. The manual was so well received that a second and now a further improved and expanded third edition has been written and is now in your hands.

Welcome to the profession of substitute teaching! People choose to be substitute teachers for a variety of reasons. Many times substitute teachers are certified teachers who are in-between jobs. Sometimes, they are college students who want teaching experience and some extra cash. Many times, substitute teachers are mothers of school age children, who want to work the same hours as their children attend school. Finally, there are some substitute teachers who are retired professionals who desire a rewarding part-time job. Whatever the reason you have for substitute teaching, you have chosen a worthy profession and as such you will want to be a professional worthy of the position.

The *Substitute Teacher's Reference Manual - Third Edition* is designed to help you, the substitute teacher, in your day to day contact with students in the classroom and to assist you in all aspects of substitute teaching. It covers such areas as getting started in the profession, understanding the psychology of young people's minds and maintaining order in the classroom. The guide also provides you with classroom-tested activities designed for various grade levels that you are welcome to photocopy and use in the classroom.

The activities in this guide are divided according to the most appropriate grade level. Do not let this prevent you from a bit of experimentation in mixing grade level activities. Sometimes, the younger students are up to the challenge of a more advanced activity, and sometimes the older students enjoy completing simple, fun, elementary activities.

There are several forms in the manual to be completed by you, which will provide you with pertinent information that applies to the various schools and/or classrooms in which you will be working. I might suggest that you make several copies of the form entitled, *Notes to the Classroom Teacher*, so that you will be able to provide a report for each teacher you stand in for during the year.

Once you have read the specific notes from the classroom teacher, use any free time you have in or between classes to read the chapters in the guide which cover classroom management, knowing your audience and maintaining order in the classroom. I hope that the ideas and approaches in the *Substitute Teacher's Reference Manual—Third Edition* help you to become a highly competent and sought after professional.

I wish to thank the many students I have taught in my role as substitute teacher for their input in the writing of this manual. If you like the materials offered in the guide and/or you have any questions or suggestions for future editions, please write me at the address on the copyright page of the book.

Carol A. Jones

_____

One

Getting Started

The criterion necessary for becoming a substitute teacher varies not only from state to state, but also from county to county within each state. In some rural areas only a high school diploma is required. In other areas, you might need to have two to four years of college in order to become a substitute teacher. In all cases, you will need to contact the county school board in the area in which you plan to work and obtain the necessary forms.

Once you have completed all the necessary paperwork for substitute teaching and have obtained your teaching certificate, you need to decide what grade level you want to teach. Some people are better suited to work with very young children, while others, myself included, prefer to work with the older student. You might need to work with various grade levels before you find your "niche".

The more familiar you are with your surroundings, the more effective you will be as a substitute teacher. For this reason, I have found that is better to limit oneself to substitute teaching in one or two schools. Also, by limiting yourself to one or two schools, you will become more familiar to both the administrators and to the students.

You should make an appointment to speak to the principal(s) of the school(s) you want to work. When you call, mention the reason for setting up the appointment—that you are now a certified substitute teacher and would like to work at his/her school. At the same time, ask who coordinates substitute teaching schedules. You should also speak to this person. When speaking to the coordinator, mention that you have an appointment with the principal and ask if it will be possible to speak with the coordinator after you meet with the principal.

Be certain to dress professionally for your appointment. You will want to make your interview with the principal short but productive. The principal of a school, while aware of all functions of the school, seldom if ever is in charge of coordinating substitute teaching schedules. You are not there to impress this person into calling you every day to work in his/her school. This meeting is twofold. First, it is a courtesy to speak with the principal of the school in which you will be working. Secondly, you will want to spend some time in the school prior to taking a substitute assignment and you will need the principal's permission and cooperation to do this. Bring a notebook and pen with you to the interview and be certain to jot down important names, asking for the correct spelling if necessary.

After you have introduced yourself, inform the principal of your intention to work in a limited number of schools. If you already know the schools in which you want you work, you might mention the names of the schools to the principal at this time. Explain that prior to taking an assignment you would appreciate the opportunity of being able to spend a day at this school, observing student and teacher activities. At this time ask for permission to do this and also ask if he/she could recommend a teacher in the school that would be willing to have you as a guest for the day. This should complete the interview. Thank the principal for his/her time and go on to your meeting with the substitute teachers' coordinator.

In this meeting, you want to present yourself as a dependable, reliable and flexible person. As a substitute teacher, you will be getting last minute calls and you must be the type of person that is ready to work at a moment's notice. Mention that you have already spoken to the principal and will be spending a day in the school to become familiar with the surroundings. It is also important that you let the coordinator know that you will be limiting yourself to accepting positions from a select number of schools.

Since this is the person who will be in charge of your employment with the school, there are a number of questions you need to ask. I would suggest you ask the following questions and add to this list any questions that you feel are important to ask. Be sure to write the answers to these questions in your notebook.

1. What are the hours of the school's operation?
2. When should I arrive? When will I leave?
3. Is there a sign in sheet?
4. Where are the teacher's mailboxes?
5. Is there a cafeteria for lunch? May I bring my own lunch?
6. What is the dress code? Is there a casual day every week? Is there a school color's day? What are the school colors?
7. Can I book substitute teaching assignments in advance?
8. What time do you begin making your calls in the morning?
9. Where should I park? Do I need a parking permit?
10. What are the procedures to follow in the event of a fire or tornado drill?

> Note: In the appendix of this manual, there is a school information section (three pages). Photo copy these forms so that you can complete one set for each school you plan to work at.

When you are done, ask if there are any open assignments at this time that need to be filled. If not, thank the coordinator for the time spent answering your questions and mention that you will check back periodically to see if there is anything available. Be certain to stop by and see the coordinator when you are in the school for your visit and again ask if there are any available assignments.

You will want to repeat this procedure at each school at which you intend to be on call as a substitute teacher. As before mentioned, one or two schools is best, but in no instance would I suggest you take on more than three. If you do this, you will lose the advantage of familiarity.

Once you have met with the principals and coordinators of your selected schools and spent a day visiting each school, you are ready to begin substitute teaching. The way to insure yourself of always having work when you want it, is to make yourself known. You want to say yes as often as possible to the coordinators when they call. If you must say no, explain why — "I have an assignment at another school, but thank you for calling and please call again."

You should stop by each school at least once a week and ask if they have any upcoming openings. The majority of times when you pre-book assignments, you will be filling in for teachers who are away at conferences or in-service meetings. These meetings are arranged weeks in advance and therefore the substitutes can be hired weeks in advance. The most important thing to remember when pre-booking dates is to not duplicate your assignments. Always carry a small calendar with you and write all your assignments clearly on the correct dates. Write down the name of the school and the teacher for which you will be substituting. There is nothing more embarrassing than showing up at the wrong school for a work assignment.

Because many school districts work off a master list for substitute teachers, you might be called by several schools to work for the day. It is up to you whether or not to accept the assignment or wait to see if one of your preferred schools calls. In no instance would I suggest that you ask another school not to ever call you, even if you cannot or do not want to work at that school. Once you are scratched off a list, it is nearly impossible to be reinstated and you never know when you might change your mind.

Another way to insure that you have as much work as you want is to have teachers ask for you by name. The way to insure that teachers request you is to always have students complete their lessons. Leave a note thanking the teacher for allowing you to supervise his/her class and to ask to be requested should he/she again be in need of a substitute. (Note: There is a *Notes to the Classroom Teacher* form in the appendix which was designed for this purpose.) Always be helpful and courteous to fellow teachers that you work with during the day. Make yourself and your qualifications known when you are with other teachers in the teachers' lounge. Introduce yourself and do not be afraid to ask other teachers to ask for you whenever they need a substitute teacher. Teachers like knowing whom they are leaving in charge of their students.

It will take a little time, but eventually you will build a "clientele" in the school system and you will have all the work you need.

Two

Your Role in the Classroom

The purpose of this chapter is to give you a format to follow in your day to day role as a substitute teacher. As a substitute teacher, your role in the classroom is to maintain order and to have the students complete any lessons that have been assigned. It is not your place, unless you are under long term assignment, to direct learning. Even if you are a certified teacher, you are not the teacher of the class in which you substitute teach.

Hopefully, you will have spent at least one day at the school before you are called in to substitute. First of all you must arrive on time. Most schools will ask that teachers and substitute teachers arrive at least one-half hour before the first class is scheduled to begin. You should check in with the substitute coordinator and sign in on a sign-in sheet if one is available. You should always dress professionally. The next step is to pick up your assignment and be certain that you know where the room is where you will be working. It is possible that the room is locked, so ask if you need a key.

Look over the teacher's schedule. Check to see if the teacher has any assigned duties. Most schools will assign duties to teachers during various parts of the school year, such as parking lot duty, lunch room duty, tardy hall duty, etc. It is important that you know what duty, if any, your teacher is responsible to perform and ask if you should cover that duty. You will usually have to stand in for the teacher in his/her assignment. The only time this would not be so is if the teacher's assignment is for tutoring. In this instance you might just be required to inform the students that there will not be a tutoring session while the teacher is absent. Do not for one moment think that you can ignore any assigned duty. If something happens in the parking lot or in the lunch room and no one is there to assist, you will be at fault for ignoring the assignment. This is not the way to insure job security.

> Note: In the appendix of this manual, there is a classroom information section (two pages). Photo copy these forms so that you can complete one set for each teacher you stand in for.

Once you understand the teacher's schedule, know where the classroom is, and are aware of any added duties, you should pick up the teacher's mail from the mailroom. Go through the mail, checking for items that pertain to the daily routine and leave any mail that is personally addressed to the teacher in the mailbox. The items that are important to you are any attendance scantrons, notices for the day and lists of student activities that might list the names of students being dismissed during the day.

With mail in hand, you can go to the classroom. The first thing you do after unlocking the room and turning on the lights is to look for the day's assignment. If the teacher planned on being absent there should be a list that explains what the teacher expects the students to do for the day. If the absence is unexpected, then the department head will probably bring in a lesson plan chosen from those that are kept on file for emergencies.

Take a look around the room to see where everything is located. Check for the office intercom. This is how the office keeps in contact with the classrooms. Take a minute and test the system. Be sure that you know how to call the office so that in case of an emergency you do not have to fumble with an unfamiliar system. Make sure that you know where all your exits are and that none of them are blocked in case an emergency evacuation is required. Pick up any items that are on the floor. Make sure all the windows are closed and that the air-conditioning or heating system is working.

The next step is to write your name on the board and the day's date. You might also want to write the day's assignment on the board for any students entering the class early. If the teacher has written the day's assignment on the board, take a moment to write the assignment down in your notebook. Students have a tendency to erase assignments off the board, especially when there is a substitute teacher. If you have the assignment written down, it will be simple enough to replace it. Also, throughout the day, check to see that page and/or chapter numbers have not been changed. This is another way that students try to get out of completing assignments. They change the assignment to one that was already completed.

Now you should visit an adjoining classroom. Introduce yourself and ask the name of the teacher next to you. At this point you might ask the teacher if you may send a student to his/her classroom should you have any discipline problems. Ask to meet the department head. Introduce yourself. If you do not have any lesson plans from the teacher, ask the department head if he/she knows where the lesson plans for your students are kept. Mention that if there are no lesson plans, you do have an assortment of lesson plans to work with (from this manual). Ask the department head the policy on giving student passes. Are the student's allowed to leave the room to go the rest room? Should you allow students to go to the media center?

Always be in your class before the bell rings and never leave your classroom before all the students have left. Be prepared. It is a good idea to have a couple of extra pencils on hand because students are many times not prepared for class. Be sure that you ask for your pencils back if you lend them out. Another necessity is a legal pad or a three-ring binder with some loose-leaf note paper inside.

Please do not bring newspapers or personal reading material to class with the intention of having something to occupy your time while the students are busy with their assignments. During this time, you should circulate the room and offer assistance to any students in need.

The first thing you want to do when the bell rings is to introduce yourself to the students. Explain that their teacher is absent for whatever reason and that you will be their substitute teacher for the day. Inform them that you do have an assignment for them and that you will give them the assignment as soon as you have taken roll. If you have a scantron attendance sheet, I would suggest that you ask one of your students to call out the student names and take attendance for you. The reason for this is that many times students do not go by their given names--other students will know how to address the student when they come across the name on the roll. This will eliminate the chance of embarrassment, for you or the student. Also, it gives you a chance to see who is responding when a name is called. You will not be able to recall all the student's names, but a few might stick. If there is no formal roll, then it is best to write the date and note the period on a piece of notebook paper and pass it around the room for the students to sign. You might ask a reliable student in the class to check the names. This roster will serve as an attendance record for the returning teacher.

At the beginning of the school year, teachers usually have seating charts so that they (regular classroom teacher) can learn the names of their students. If a seating chart is available, it will be a great resource for you. Unfortunately, one of two things usually happens regarding the seating chart. One–it is no longer necessary for the regular teacher to maintain a seating plan because he/she knows the students' names and the students now sit where ever they choose. Two–you cannot find the seating chart and the students are sitting wherever they choose.

It is important for you to be able to call students by name. It not only breeds familiarity, but in the case of a discipline problem, it is difficult to reprimand a student if you have to ask the student his/her name first. If there is no seating plan available, you can quickly learn the student's names by playing a round robin activity before the lesson begins.

> Note: In the appendix of this manual, there is a seating chart, which you can use as a sign-up and also as an attendance sheet. Be sure to make several copies of this form so that you will have blank ones ready for each class you teach.

You will want to maintain a journal during the day to leave for the teacher. Some of the items you should note are any excused absence notes that the students give you, any students that were particularly helpful and any incidents that happened that you feel the teacher should know about. Sometimes a particular assignment cannot be completed because one of the necessary elements is not available. For example, the teacher may have wanted the students to watch a film and write a commentary on the content, but the VCR did not work. Or the teacher might have given an assignment that required the students use the daily newspaper, but the paper was never delivered. In any case, if a situation such as this arises, be sure to document it so that the students are not held responsible for work that they could not finish and you are not to blame for an assignment not completed. You will want to end your note to the teacher on a positive note. Thank him/her for allowing you to supervise the class and tell the teacher that you would value the opportunity to substitute teach for him/her at any time in the future and would appreciate being requested for the post. Again, you can use the *Notes to the Classroom Teacher* form that is in the appendix for this purpose.

Never leave the classroom unattended. If an emergency arises and you have a classroom that adjoins another room, explain your situation to the neighboring teacher and ask if the teacher could watch your class for a few minutes. If you do not have another teacher nearby, call the office and ask for an administrator to come to your room. When the administrator arrives, explain your situation and ask for class coverage so that you can leave the room.

You may be asked to substitute teach for a regular teacher who has the aide of a para-professional or co-teacher in the classroom. Should this situation occur, discuss your role with the para-professional or co-teacher before the class begins. Sometimes it is best for you to assume the role of regular teacher and allow the para-professional or co-teacher to continue their normal routine. At other times, the regular teacher may have instructed the para-professional or co-teacher to lead the class. In such a case you will assume the role of the para-professional or co-teacher.

For the most part you will find the para-professional in the exceptional student classroom. Exceptional students are those students who have a physical or learning disability that necessitates special education services. Below is a list of various exceptional student categories and a brief description of each category:

Educable Mentally Handicapped–Students of below average

intelligence who need additional classroom support because they

are unable to progress at a normal classroom pace

Emotionally Handicapped–Students whose emotional and or behavioral

problems prevent them from yielding average performance in the

classroom

Gifted/Talented–Students of superior intelligence who are able to

progress through conventional courses at a faster than normal pace

Physically Impaired–Students whose physical disabilities require special

assistance and/or equipment

Sensory Impaired–Students with hearing and/or visual handicaps

Severely Handicapped–Students with severe and/or multiple handicaps

who have limited practical and social skills

Specific Learning Disabilities–Students who are not working up to the

level of their abilities

Speech and/or Language Impaired–Students who have difficulties

with oral communication skills

Should you be asked to substitute teach in an exceptional student classroom and

you do not have a para-professional or co-teacher in the class, do not feel ill at ease. For

the most part the exceptional student classroom environment will be very much like a

regular classroom environment. The exception being that the class size is usually smaller

and the lessons are more detailed. The most important thing to remember if you

substitute teach in an exceptional student classroom, is that you need to use an extra measure of understanding, compassion and above all patience. But then, these qualities will serve you well in all classrooms.

During lunch period, visit with the other teachers. This is a wonderful opportunity to listen—not talk. Do not offer any negative comments about what may have transpired in your classroom during the morning classes. If you cannot make a positive comment, then make no comments at all. Once you have gotten to know the teachers a little better, you will want to ask them to request you, should they require a substitute teacher in the future.

At the end of the school day, you should look around the room and pick up any debris that is on the floor or on the desks. Make sure that the windows are closed and locked. Turn out the lights and lock the door behind you. Bring all the completed assignments and the notes for the teacher with you to the mailroom and place them in the teacher's mailbox. Sign out for the day and return the room key to the coordinator's office.

Three
_____

Knowing Your Audience

You do not have to be a child psychologist to substitute teach, but it does help to have a basic understanding of adolescent psychology before you enter the classroom. Children's behavior and the way in which you relate to children depend upon which age group you work with. Earlier in this guide, I suggested that you might want to concentrate your substitute teaching into a particular area — elementary, middle school, or high school. As you read this section, it will become clear to you why that is a good proposition. The more experienced you become in handling a particular age group, the more of a professional you will become. If you feel comfortable in a situation, your students will be comfortable and everyone involved will benefit from your expertise.

When discussing the elementary student, one must really consider two distinct age groups — the very young child that attends kindergarten through third grades and the older child that attends grades four through six. The youngest group of elementary children, grades kindergarten through third grade will look to you as a surrogate parent. Many of these children are away from their parents for the very first time. They will vary in maturity more than any other age group and you need to have a nurturing personality if you want to work with this age group.

These little ones will come in to you first thing in the morning and let you know exactly what is on their mind. They are hungry, tired and they did not have time to comb their hair before school. They need you to tie their shoes, straighten out their clothes and look at the hole in their mouths where they lost a tooth last night. These youngest students are accustomed to having the undivided attention of their parents, so it is difficult for them to wait for even a minute while you attend to another child. You need to be able to go in thirty directions at once, without blinking an eye or losing a beat.

These little ones are also a bit difficult to keep on task. You might have to give them directions two or three times before they understand the assignment. Then you will need to check with each child individually to be certain that he or she does indeed understand the assignment. These tiny students will love you. They will want to hug you while you are talking to another student. They will grab your clothing as you walk by, so that you will stay close. They want you to hold their hand while you walk to the lunchroom. If you are a touchy-feely person, then this age group is for you!

The second age group in the elementary school environment is the child that attends grades four through six. This is an age of experimentation. The children still respect authority, but they are spreading their wings. For the most part they do not mean to be mischievous, it is just part of their nature at this age.

Unlike the kindergarten to third grade group of children, the fourth to sixth grade group of children will not be quite so needy. They come to school pretty much prepared to start the day. They are dressed, their hair is combed and their shoes are tied. They do not crave the affection that the younger child craves, but they do still want the attention. This age group will do anything and everything to get your attention. They want to "do things" for you. "Can I erase the board?" "Can I clean the erasers?" "Can I empty the wastebaskets?" "Can I bring that to the office for you?" They also need constant approval. You should look at their work carefully and make specific comments. "That's nice," is not enough of a comment for a child this age. You need to make a more definite comment like, "I like the way you used red and orange on the leaves and outlined them in brown. They really stand out."

While most teachers find the fourth grade to sixth grade students to be the easiest group of students to work with, do not assume that these students are in any way mature. This is a very deceiving age group. They act all grown up, but they are still very young and very naive. They will do the most foolish and sometimes dangerous acts, not because they are being naughty, but because they are very immature and just do not know any better. If you want to work with elementary students, whether they are the littlest ones or the older group, the most important requirement is that you have "eyes behind your head." You must always be on the alert and never let down your defense. You are the guardian of some very important chattel.

The next students to be addressed are middle school students. Some school districts have middle schools that include grades six through eight. Other districts have middle schools or junior high schools that include grades seven through nine. Therefore, the age group being addressed in this section includes students that attend grades six through nine.

When you teach in a middle school environment, you will sometimes be confused as to just where you really are. Some classes might look as if elementary students are in the room and others might look as if high school students have come to middle school for the day. Most likely, you will have classes where half the students look younger than their age and half the students look older.

Middle school students are growing by leaps and bounds. Their hormones are exploding in all directions and they have little if any ambition to learn anything. The girls are interested in boys and the boys are interested in discovering why the girls are so interested in them. Middle school girls write notes, fix their hair -- with hair spray, and put on make-up all day long. Middle school boys break pencils, throw spit balls and play with each other's baseball caps all day long.

This is an age when the students still respect authority. They also think they can get away with all the things they got away with as little children. They are not sure whether they should act "cute" or grown up. Many times the girls will talk baby-talk with one another at the same time that they are putting on grown-up eye shadow. The boys will practice making "noises" with their armpits like little children while they discuss yesterday's baseball game as though they were a group of grown men. This age group is full of energy and you need to also be full of energy if you want to be successful in teaching middle school students. Middle school students are funnier, sweeter and more entertaining than any other age group, but they will keep you on your toes!

High school students change dramatically between the time they enter the ninth grade and the time they graduate as twelfth graders. Ninth grade students are ready to take on the world--teachers included. They challenge authority in everything they do. They are "grown-up" and no longer feel that they need anyone to tell them what they can and cannot do. They can decide everything on their own. No one, especially an adult, can tell them what to do. They know what subjects will be useful to them in life and which ones are "a waste of time". For example, according to most ninth graders, Algebra is a subject that, "I will never use in my life." They also feel as though they will never need History, English or Social Studies. Art is usually accepted as a necessity of life.

Ninth grade girls are always busy trying to catch the attention of tenth grade boys. Ninth grade boys are hiding out for a year until they are tenth grade boys–old enough for ninth grade girls to like them. Toward the end of the ninth grade, you start to see some maturing in these students, because once the novelty of being a high school student has worn thin, they begin to think about career and college possibilities.

Tenth grade students are, in my estimation, God's gift to teachers. There are a number of reasons for this. They are in most cases too young to drive a car or have a job. Therefore, they still have time to do their homework. They are constantly thinking about the opposite sex, but are still too young to date. They tend to spend time with their boyfriends or girlfriends in the library–studying or working on school projects. It is so much easier to get a parent's permission to study with a member of the opposite sex than it is to get permission to go on a date at this age.

Tenth graders also are quite serious about college. They still have a chance to bring up their grades to be able to get into the college of their choice. They are also considering what they might do for work once they are old enough to get a job. They are pretty much over the hostile phase of challenging adults so if they choose not to do something, they just do not do it–no fuss. Tenth graders are for the most part content in their same sex friendships and not yet thinking of their boy/girl relationships in terms of marriage. Because of this, they are more easy going and carefree than other high school students.

Eleventh graders will probably be your most attentive students. At no time in their life will students be more concerned about their grades than when they are in the eleventh grade. School counselors have told them for years that, "Colleges look at your eleventh grade transcripts." Eleventh graders are actively choosing their colleges and taking SATs (Scholastic Aptitude Tests). They have chosen their classes and by this time have weeded out the courses they cannot handle and have the courses they truly need or truly want.

Most boys and girls are actively dating at this time and because of this they are usually on their best behavior with one another in the classroom. Students are no longer embarrassed to sit near someone of the opposite sex that they like. In fact, they often make a point of requesting these seats. The boys are becoming young men and you will notice their social manners reflecting this change. They will hold doors open for the young ladies and will offer to get books or other items for the girls, just to be polite.

One distinct change that you will notice with eleventh graders and will continue to notice with twelfth graders, is that many times they come to school exhausted. By the eleventh grade, some students have part-time jobs. Combine this with an active social life, home life and school and there is little time left to sleep. Often, students will fall asleep in class. Be understanding of this situation and wake them up without berating them. Some of these students must work to help support their families and they are having a difficult time meeting all the commitments that are placed upon their young lives.

Finally we have the twelfth graders. In the beginning of the school year, they are very much like the eleventh graders in their personality and their actions. Toward the end of the year they live in a world of their own. This is understandable. They are getting ready to leave their cocoons and venture out into the world as young adults. While it is exciting for some, for many of these students it is a very scary situation.

There will be students in your senior class that have lived in the same area all their lives. Because of this, they have had the same friends around them for the last twelve to thirteen years. Now that they are seniors, they realize that they are about to lose the closeness of this camaraderie and will soon be outside the school environment, having to make new friends for the first time in their lives. For thirteen years, there has been a place for them to go to every day–school. Soon they will no longer have school as a safe haven or retreat. They are going to either go off to college or they must find work and be able to support themselves.

Many graduating students will be going into the military. Some will enter because they want to, but others will enlist because they have no other choice. They cannot afford college and they do not have the necessary skills to make enough money to support themselves. Twelfth graders are often seriously thinking about marriage. High school sweethearts that have dated throughout their high school years now feel that it is time to get married. When young people have such major life decisions to make, it is little wonder that their minds are not on school work. If you find yourself teaching seniors, please be considerate of their adult problems and treat them accordingly.

Whether you teach the five-year-old kindergarten student or the eighteen-year-old high school senior, do so with compassion. Understanding the psychology of children as they move from one stage of adolescence to another is an important step in your becoming a professional substitute teacher. This understanding will come with time if you employ careful observation and seek to recognize the unique personalities of each age group. When you are employed as a substitute teacher, the well-being of these children is in your hands. It is important that you do not take this assignment lightly and that you give the position all the significance that it rightly deserves.

_____

Four

Maintaining Order in the Classroom

The ultimate goal you should have as a substitute teacher is the ability to maintain order in the classroom while the students complete their assignments. Maintaining order is the same thing as achieving good discipline. In fact, once you are able to maintain order in the classroom, you will rarely need to discipline a student. This is good because formal discipline should be left to regular teachers and not be the responsibility of substitute teachers.

The approach you use to maintain order in elementary school is somewhat different from the method you will use in the upper grades. As you read in the chapter entitled, *Knowing Your Audience*, elementary students are still pretty good about respecting the authority of adults. This will help you in your endeavor to control the classroom environment.

The best way to maintain order in the elementary classroom is to keep the students busy and/or entertained. I never go into an elementary school class without a packet of activities and a selection of children's books. The books I bring are books that I have purchased at flea markets and yard sales. I always have the books approved by the school librarian before I bring them into the classroom. Note: A sample of a book approval form can be found in the Appendix.

The elementary student loves to be read to, but you should read books that have plenty of pictures to show to the students. Read slowly and put a great deal of emotion (acting) into your reading. Some wonderful books that I have used in the elementary classroom are:

Ehrlich, Amy, editor. The Random House Book of Fairy Tales. New York: Random House, 1985.

Koss, Amy Goldman. Where Fish Go In Winter. Los Angeles: Price Stern Sloan, 1987. (poetry)

Marshall, Edward. Three By The Sea. New York: Dial Books for Young Readers, 1981.

Silverstein, Shel. Where the Sidewalk Ends. New York: Harper Collins, 1974. (poetry)

Winter, Milo, illustrator. The Aesop for Children. New York: Checkerboard Press, 1947.

Should you have a behavior problem in your elementary school classroom, I suggest the following line of action. First, try time out. Ask the student(s) to move to a remote area of the classroom. If this does not resolve the problem, send the child to a neighboring teacher's classroom. (In the section, *Your Role in the Classroom*, it was suggested that you prearrange this option with another teacher before the school day begins.) If you encounter a serious behavior problem that requires immediate intervention, use the intercom button to call for a school administrator. At no time should you use physical force of any kind to restrain or separate students in any grade level.

Middle school students will test you to see if they can catch you off guard. Remember that it is important to be friendly with the students without being a friend to them. You must gain and retain their respect. The way to do this is to let them know from the start that if they respect you, you will respect them. Let the students know that if you all work together, both the students and you will have a pleasant day.

Again, the key to maintaining order in the classroom is to limit the amount of free time the students have. Whenever possible, I try to conduct lessons with the whole class, rather than having them work alone or in pairs. If there is a reading assignment, we read it as a class. There are a number of entertaining ways you can lead a whole class reading session. Here are two examples to use in middle school classrooms:

SPEED READING - Inform the students that they have a long reading assignment. If they would prefer to finish it in class, rather then bring it home for homework, they can take turns speed reading. The rules to this activity are simple. Only students who volunteer will read. Readers will read as fast as they can, but they must read each section loud and clear. Each reader will read two paragraphs before someone else takes a turn, but students can volunteer to read more than once. Note: You should speed read the first one or two paragraphs as an example.

SPIRIT READING - In this reading activity, students take turns reading, when the spirit "moves" them. Students do not actively volunteer to read, they just begin reading when another student stops. A student cannot read more than two paragraphs at a time, but the spirit can "move" a student more then once. You might experience a few moments of silence, or even have to spirit read once or twice yourself. This activity will take some patience on your part, but it really is a fun reading experience for the students.

You might also consider bringing books into the middle school classroom. Middle school students would rather read and act out the stories for each other, than be read to. Remember to have your books approved by the school or else you can pick up a book or two from the media center before class. These are some of the books I

recommend for the middle school classroom:

Aiken, Joan. Past Eight O'Clock, Goodnight Stories. New York: Viking

Penguin, 1987.

Cecil, Laura, editor. Stuff and Nonsense. New York: Greenwillow Books, 1989.

Scieszka, Jon. The True Story of The 3 Little Pigs! New York: Viking Penguin,

1989.

Silverstein, Shel. Where the Sidewalk Ends. New York: Harper Collins, 1974.

(poetry)

Winter, Milo, illustrator. The Aesop for Children. New York: Checkerboard

Press, 1947.

If you should encounter a difficult discipline problem in your middle school class,

handle it in the same manner as was suggested for an elementary school discipline

problem—first, time out, next, transfer the student to another classroom and, in the case of

an emergency, call the office. In middle school you might encounter a fight between

students. If this happens and you cannot get the students to stop with verbal commands,

isolate them from the rest of the students, call the office and keep your distance until

qualified help arrives.

As a high school substitute teacher, you will more likely than not be supervising

classroom assignments that you will not be able to complete yourself. For example, I am

certified to teach English, so when I was placed in a high school Chemistry class, I was a

fish out of water. For this reason, I suggest that unless the teacher left specific

instructions that prohibit the students from working together, you allow them to work in pairs. This way, they can help each other with the problems. Be sure to note in your journal to the teacher that you allowed students to work in pairs and your reason for doing so.

There will be times when you will be asked to substitute for a high school teacher and are left without an assignment. Again, for this reason it is important to be prepared with activities suitable for the high school student and also to have some reading material on hand. High school students, like elementary students like to be read to. The following books are books that I have successfully used in the high school classroom:

Asimov, Isaac, editor. Young Monsters. New York: Harper & Row, 1985.

Gordon, Ruth, sel. Under All Silences: Shades of Love. New York: Harper & Row, 1987. (poetry)

Scieszka, Jon. The True Story of The 3 Little Pigs! New York: Viking Penguin, 1989.

Silverstein, Shel. Where the Sidewalk Ends. New York: Harper Collins, 1974. (poetry)

Sturrock, Walt, illustrator. Ghost Stories. Morris Plains, NJ: Unicorn Publishing House, Inc.: 1989.

Most high school discipline problems can be nipped in the bud with the proper use of body language. Direct, steady eye contact, a firm verbal directive or just a stroll over to the disruptive area, should do the trick. If not, do not waste time or energy on the student—send him/her to a neighboring room. If a student is excessively disruptive, call the office on the intercom and inform them that you are sending a student (give name) to the office for disrupting your classroom. You are not a failure if you do not prevent all disruptive behavior. But, you are not a professional if you allow disruptive students to control the classroom environment.

In any classroom you need to set the tone for the class within the first five minutes. The best way to maintain order in the classroom is to prevent discipline problems from arising in the first place. It is important to begin classroom activities as soon as possible. If you take the time to take attendance, let the students chat with friends or run to their lockers, you will lose momentum and it might be difficult, if not impossible to regain control. Get into the assignment immediately. Take role after the class is settled down and absorbed in their work.

Set limits, but do not threaten students. Never make threats that you are not prepared to back up. If you tell a student that you will give him/her one more opportunity to behave before you send the student out of the room and the student misbehaves again, send the student to another room. If you make idle threats, it will not be long before the students take control of the classroom.

Keep in mind that whatever grade level you teach, maintaining order in the classroom should be as simple as having dinner with friends. Set a respectful tone at the beginning of class and maintain composure at all times. Once you lose your patience and react emotionally by shouting or pleading for compliance, you will have lost the respect of the students and it will be impossible for you to regain control. When a discipline problem arises, take a deep breath, remember you are in charge and take whatever measures are necessary to calmly resolve the problem.

Five

Introduction to Student Activities

In the ideal situation, you will walk into a classroom, find a detailed lesson plan of what the students are expected to do and the students will spend the entire period quietly completing the assignment. Unfortunately, this is not always the case. There will be instances when the teacher is unable to leave a detailed lesson plan. Sometimes you will get a week-long assignment and the students will finish their work in three days, leaving two days where there is no assignment.

If the teacher has left a lesson plan, be certain to have the students complete the assignment. If for any reason you find yourself in a classroom without a lesson plan, the following activities will help you manage your class in a useful and productive manner. Be certain to leave a copy of the activity you use, along with the students' responses, for the classroom teacher.

The following activities are divided into three sections: elementary level, middle school level and high school level. Because of the great differences in ability between elementary students, this section has been broken up into two parts; Kindergarten through grade three and grade four through grade six. In some school districts, middle school consists of grades six, seven and eight. Other districts have junior high schools that are composed of seventh, eighth and ninth grades. Therefore the middle school activities are geared toward students ranging in grade levels, six through nine. The high school activities are for students in the ninth through twelfth grades.

It is a good idea to have prizes available for some of the student activity games. You can collect free prizes throughout the year. Whenever you go to home or trade shows, pick up a few extra pencils, pens, rulers and posters. Many times if you explain that you are a school teacher, the booth operators will give you handfuls of free items. Another idea for prizes is sample vials of cologne from department stores. Leftover Halloween candies also make good prizes.

Another avenue you can explore is to ask local fast food restaurants if they give out coupons for a free hamburger, order of fries, soft drink, etc. to be used as a classroom reward for deserving students. Also, ask the same of local movie theaters–free passes, coupons for popcorn, etc. Many places such as these will be more than happy to accommodate you.

You will find that several of the middle school activities can be used with high school students and vice versa. I would suggest that you try each activity first with the grade level for which it is intended and become comfortable with conducting the activity before you attempt to use it with a different grade level. All of the activities should take a full class period (fifty to sixty minutes) to complete. You can modify them if you need to lengthen or shorten the time required for the exercise.

I encourage you to photocopy these activities for use in the classroom. Also, feel free to reconstruct and/or embellish the activities.

ELEMENTARY - KINDERGARTEN THROUGH GRADE THREE
ACTIVITY ONE

THE ALPHABET BOOK

Note: Youngest students can make the book for their own use. Older students can make the book to give as a gift to a kindergarten or first grade class.

1. Assign each student a page to make for the "Alphabet Book"

2. The student will put the letter in both upper and lower case at the top of the page. Next the student will draw and color a picture of an object that begins with the letter. Finally the student will write the word at the bottom of the page. Note: You will need to help the younger students with the spelling.

3. If you have more than twenty-six students, you can have some students work on the cover or have students work in pairs. If you have less than twenty-six students, some students can make an extra page or you can complete the extra page(s).

4. When all the pages are complete, staple or tie the pages together with ribbons and the students will have a class book that they made themselves.

Variation: Instead of drawing pictures, students can find pictures in magazines and paste them onto the pages.

A a

Apple

ELEMENTARY - KINDERGARTEN THROUGH GRADE THREE
ACTIVITY TWO

GUESS WHAT I FOUND?   GUESSING GAME

1. Teacher should lead the game. Tell the students, "I am looking around the room and I found something square. What did I find?"

2. Students take turns guessing what the object is:

> Did you find a square door?
> > No, I did not find a square door.
> Did you find a square desk?
> > No, I did not find a square desk.
> Did you find a square floor tile?
> > Yes, I found a square floor tile.

3. The first student to guess the correct object chooses a new shape and object. Some examples around the classroom that you can use are:

> Circle - intercom speaker
> Rectangle - light switch
> Square - bulletin board
> Oval - clock
> Square - television
> Rectangle - video cassette recorder

4. Try to encourage all the students to guess so that everyone gets a chance to play both parts. Students can guess more than once but they can only choose a new shape/object one time until everyone has had a chance to play.

Note: Instead of shapes, you can also use a color category. For example, "I am looking around the room and I found something red. What did I find?

ELEMENTARY - KINDERGARTEN THROUGH GRADE THREE
ACTIVITY THREE

THE NAME GAME

1. Give each student a sheet of paper and show him or her how to fold it into ten boxes.

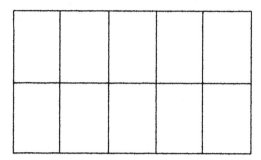

2. Have the students put one letter from their names in each one of the squares. You may need to help the younger students with this. It is also a good idea to put an example of the activity on the board.

C	A	R	M	E
L	A	.	.	.

3. Have the students draw a picture in each square using the letter in the picture. Again, it is a good idea to put an example on the board. The letter "C" for example can be closed off to make a face and a hat can be placed on top of the letter. Empty boxes can be used for any type of freestyle design.

**ELEMENTARY - KINDERGARTEN THROUGH GRADE THREE
ACTIVITY FOUR**

ROUND ROBIN MEMORY GAME

1. Students should puts desks/chairs in a circle.

2. Students will take turns saying what their name is and also their favorite food that begins with the letter of their first name. For example:

"My name is Crystal and I like <u>c</u>andy".

3. Each student must say the names and food items of all the students that had turns before them.

1st Student:	My name is Crystal and I like <u>c</u>andy.
2nd Student:	Crystal likes <u>c</u>andy. My name is Tommy and I like <u>t</u>omatoes.
3rd Student:	Crystal likes <u>c</u>andy. Tommy likes <u>t</u>omatoes. My name is Billy and I like <u>b</u>ananas.
4th Student:	Crystal likes <u>c</u>andy. Tommy likes <u>t</u>omatoes. Billy likes <u>b</u>ananas. My name is Mike and I like <u>m</u>elons.

The game continues all around the circle. Note: You might want to keep a written list of students' names and their food choices in case you have to jog other students' memories.

This is a great game to play with students if you want to become familiar with their names.

**ELEMENTARY - KINDERGARTEN THROUGH GRADE THREE
ACTIVITY FIVE**

CREATE A BIRTHDAY CARD

1. Give each student a sheet of paper that is folded into four squares. (Use the template on bottom of page.)

2. Draw the following diagrams on the board to show students how the card will look before and after it is folded. Also show them a hand-held example.

3. Have the students print "Happy Birthday" and draw a design on Box #1 (cover).

4. Students can write their own greeting on Box #3 (inside right). Write a suggested greeting on the front board.

CHANGE-A-WORD STORY

The following story has certain words and/or phrases written in **BOLD CAPS**. These words make no sense in the story and need to be replaced with different words. There are no right or wrong answers. All the students will have different stories when they are finished. At the end of the activity, have the students share their stories with the rest of the class.

The Turtle Story

Once upon a time, there was a turtle named **BOZO**. **BOZO** was a **FAT** turtle

that lived in the **LAMP**. When it was hot outside, **BOZO** liked to **PLAY IN THE**

SNOW. **BOZO** had lots of **STONES** to play with. The names of his **STONES**

were, **STICKY**, **STINKY** and **YUCKY**. Every day **BOZO** and his **STONES**

would go to the **MOON** and they would play with the **APPLES** in the pond. **BOZO**

and his **STONES** loved living and playing in the **LAMP**.

THE END

HOP TO IT!

NAME _____   **DATE** _____

NEXT TO EACH WORD, WRITE THE WORD FROM THE LIST OF WORDS THAT RHYME.

boy	can	dog	fit	goat
hat	mice	pen	run	sing

1. hit _____

2. ring _____

3. fun _____

4. hen _____

5. frog _____

6. nice _____

7. toy _____

8. man _____

9. bat _____

10. coat _____

CIRCLE THE MISSPELLED SPELLING WORD. WRITE THE SPELLING WORD CORRECTLY ON THE LINE.

1. The little bay likes to play baseball.   _____

2. Con you come out to play today?   _____

3. I taught my dag a new trick today.   _____

4. My new shoes do not fot me, they are too big.   _____

5. I saw a baby goot at the petting zoo.   _____

6. The wind blew my hit off my head.   _____

7. I like the story about the three blind mace.   _____

8. Should I write with a pin or a pencil?   _____

9. If you rin, you might fall down.   _____

10. Can you seng a song for me?   _____

COMING TOGETHER

NAME _____   DATE _____

WRITE THE MISSING SPELLING WORD NEXT TO EACH SENTENCE.

ant	candy	jump	mouse	orange
ball	girl	little	nice	party

1. In the morning I like to drink _____ juice with my breakfast.

2. Tommy threw the _____, but Susie did not catch it.

3. Billy invited everyone in our class to his birthday _____.

4. Yesterday, I saw an _____ bringing food to the ant hill.

5. I like Mrs. Smith, because she is always _____ to me.

6. My mother tells me to brush my teeth after I eat _____.

7. My cat likes to chase every _____ he sees.

8. My brother is big, but my sister is _____.

9. The new _____ in our class is very pretty.

10. Tina is going to _____ rope with us after school

BUILDING SNOWMEN

NAME _____   DATE _____

WRITE EACH ADDITION PROBLEM ON THE SNOWMAN WHO HAS THE CORRECT ANSWER ON HIS TUMMY.

7 + 8	6 + 6	8 + 8	4 + 9	6 + 8
5 + 9	7 + 5	6 + 7	9 + 6	7 + 9

12

13

14

15

16

ELEMENTARY - KINDERGARTEN THROUGH GRADE THREE
ACTIVITY TEN

A DAY AT SCHOOL

NAME _____   DATE _____

WRITE A STORY, OR DRAW A PICTURE ABOUT WHAT A DAY AT SCHOOL IS LIKE FOR YOU.

My School Day

_____

_____

_____

_____

_____

_____

_____

_____

THE END

ELEMENTARY - KINDERGARTEN THROUGH GRADE THREE
ACTIVITY ELEVEN

MY FAMILY

NAME _____   DATE _____

DRAW A PICTURE OF YOUR FAMILY IN THE BOX.   THEN ANSWER THE QUESTIONS.

1. How many people are there in your family? _____

2. Who is the oldest person in your family? _____

3. Who is the youngest person in your family? _____

4. Who is the tallest person in your family? _____

5. Who is the shortest person in your family? _____

6. Where does your family live? _____

7. What does your family do for fun? _____

WHAT MAKES A SENTENCE A SENTENCE?

NAME _____   DATE _____

**EVERY SENTENCE MUST HAVE A NOUN - A PERSON, PLACE OR THING.
EVERY SENTENCE MUST ALSO HAVE A VERB - AN ACTION WORD.**

**IN EACH OF THE FOLLOWING SENTENCES, CIRCLE ALL OF THE NOUNS,
AND DRAW A LINE UNDER THE VERBS.**

1. Every day Susan and Billy play ball in the park.

2. The lion at the zoo roared when the children came too close to him.

3. The boys ran very quickly to get to the bus.

4. Mike sang a song for the teacher's holiday party.

5. Christine jumped higher than any other girl did in her class.

6. The Tampa Bay Buccaneers won every game they played.

7. The ice on the sidewalk melted very quickly.

8. The clouds in the sky floated by us while we laid on the grass.

9. The racecar driver drove his car very fast.

10. Bobby and Jane played hopscotch on the sidewalk.

11. The janitor cleaned the room after we left.

12. The leaves fell from the tree when the wind began to blow.

13. The teacher read a book to her class.

14. The ice cream melted before we could eat it.

15. David covered his hot dog with mustard.

ELEMENTARY - KINDERGARTEN THROUGH GRADE THREE
ACTIVITY THIRTEEN

THE FIVE "W'S" OF STORYTELLING

NAME _____   **DATE** _____

READ EACH SENTENCE. WRITE A WORD OR WORDS TO ANSWER THE QUESTIONS - WHO? WHAT? WHEN? WHERE? AND WHY?

1.   My friend _____ had a birthday party.

     I went to her party with my other friend _____.

2.   The present I brought to the party was a _____.

     We ate _____ and _____ at the party.

3.   The party started at _____.

     The party was on this day of the week, _____.

4.   My friend had her party at _____.

     My friend's mother bought her cake at _____.

5.   I went to the party because _____.

     I had fun at the party because _____.

A "WHALE" OF A STORY

NAME _____   DATE _____

DO YOU KNOW THE DIFFERENCE BETWEEN BIG, BIGGER AND BIGGEST?

WRITE THE CORRECT WORD ON THE LINE.

big   1. My brother caught a _____ fish than I caught.

bigger   2. The _____ animal in the sea is a whale.

biggest   3. The fish I caught was so _____ it broke the fishing line.

tall   1. The _____ boy was the best basketball player.

taller   2. Suzy was short, so all her friends were _____ than her.

tallest   3. Billy wants to be as _____ as his father when he grows up.

bright   1. The moon was _____ last night.

brighter   2. I made a wish upon the _____ star in the sky.

brightest   3. The stars in the north are _____ than the stars in the south.

PUT ALL YOUR DUCKS IN A ROW

NAME _____   DATE _____

WRITE THE FOLLOWING SENTENCES IN ORDER SO THAT THEY TELL A STORY.

When the ducks were finished eating, they went home and so did we.

At the park, we saw a duck family playing in the pond.

One day, my mother took my brother Tommy and me to the park.

We fed bread crumbs to the ducks because they were hungry.

A Day at the Park

_____

_____

_____

_____

_____

_____

THE MEANING OF WORDS

NAME _____   DATE _____

WORD MEANINGS

another   every   jolly   nothing   smart

candle   great   little   real   winter

WRITE THE CORRECT SPELLING WORDS ON THE LINE NEXT TO THE MEANING.

1. One more   _____

2. Happy or cheerful   _____

3. Knowing a lot   _____

4. Something good and terrific   _____

5. Something small   _____

6. The cold time of the year   _____

7. Each one, all of them   _____

8. None   _____

9. Made of wax, you use it for light   _____

10. Not make-believe   _____

ADDING NUMBERS

NAME _____   DATE _____

ADD EACH PAIR OF NUMBERS AND WRITE THE ANSWER UNDER THE LINE

8 +4	3 +4	6 +7	1 +4	2 +4	7 +4
7 +9	9 +7	4 +3	5 +5	5 +6	1 +5
9 +8	3 +9	8 +7	4 +1	9 +1	9 +6
6 +7	4 +5	3 +8	4 +1	9 +8	7 +4
8 +8	7 +7	5 +5	8 +6	5 +9	9 +3
3 +5	7 +3	1 +7	4 +6	7 +7	5 +7

COMPOUND MADNESS

NAME _____   DATE _____

MAKE COMPOUND WORDS USING THE WORDS FROM THE BREADBOX
AND THE WORDS ON THE LINES.

box	corn
book	top
bag	spoon
cloth	board
mat	light

1. bread _____

2. stove _____

3. pop _____

4. table _____

5. place _____

6. cook _____

7. lunch _____

8. tea _____

9. cup _____

10. flash _____

WRITING COMPLETE SENTENCES

NAME _____   DATE _____

A COMPLETE SENTENCE HAS A NOUN (a person place or thing) AND A VERB (an action word).

A COMPLETE SENTENCE BEGINS WITH A CAPITAL LETTER.

WRITE THREE COMPLETE SENTENCES ABOUT THE PICTURE.

1._____

_____

2._____

_____

3._____

_____

MY STORY

NAME _____   **DATE** _____

This is what I look like.
(Draw a picture of yourself)

This is what my family looks like.
(Draw a picture of your family)

This is what my house looks like.
(Draw a picture of your house)

This is what I want to be when I grow up.
(Draw a picture of what you want to be)

**ELEMENTARY - GRADE FOUR THROUGH GRADE SIX
ACTIVITY ONE**

WHAT'S MY LINE? - GAME SHOW

Note: Students can do this activity in small groups or as a whole class.

1. Prepare index cards with different professions and pass out one card to each student. Here are some suggested professions:

Firefighter	Baker
Doctor	Football Player
Teacher	Taxi Cab Driver
Astronaut	Carpenter

2. The "mystery guest" comes to the front of the class and performs actions (pantomime) that gives the class clues as to what job the mystery guest has.

3. The students then take turns asking questions of the guest. The guest can only answer "yes" or "no" to the first five questions. If by that time no one has guessed the profession, then the students can ask questions that require more detailed answers. Some sample yes/no questions are:

"Do you have a dangerous job"?

"Do you wear a uniform"?

"Do you work as a member of a team"?

"Are you a football player"?

4. A variation of this game is to have the students choose their own profession and write a short paragraph about what they "do" in their job. They can read the paragraph to the class after their profession has been exposed.

ELEMENTARY - GRADE FOUR THROUGH GRADE SIX
ACTIVITY TWO

CHARADES - CREATIVE DRAMA

Write each of the following items on separate cards or pieces of paper. Have each student choose a card. Students then take turns describing the item to the rest of the class using pantomime. The first student to guess the item, is the next student to come to the front of the class and perform.

POSTAGE STAMP	CD PLAYER
TEA POT	BANANA
STAPLER	TOY TRUCK
REMOTE CONTROL	WHEEL BARREL
PICTURE FRAME	BAND-AID
GARDEN HOSE	WEIGHT SCALE
BARBELLS	HOUSE COAT
SANDALS	PLAYING CARDS
HOUR GLASS	COFFEE POT
PICNIC BASKET	PIZZA CUTTER
VITAMIN PILL	POTATO CHIP
TWEEZERS	DOLLAR BILL
CHRISTMAS TREE	TELEVISION SET
TEDDY BEAR	RECORD PLAYER
BLANKET	TAXI CAB
BRICK	BRIEF CASE
YARD STICK	MICROWAVE OVEN
RADAR DETECTOR	BOOK END
TOASTER	MIRROR
BASEBALL	HAIR BRUSH

ELEMENTARY - GRADE FOUR THROUGH GRADE SIX
ACTIVITY THREE

THE AWARD SHOW

1. Students will think of an award that they would like to give to someone. The award can be for a special talent, for a special occasion, for a specific deed or for a silly reason.

2. Students should design the award and then write the inscription. Note: You might want to put an example on the board.

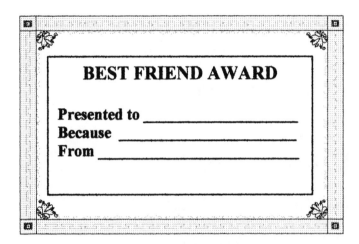

3. Allow students enough time to design, color and inscribe their awards.

4. If you have enough time in class, the students can have an awards ceremony. If the person the award is for is in class, the designer can present it to the award recipient. If the recipient is not in class, another student can accept the award on behalf of the recipient.

ELEMENTARY - GRADE FOUR THROUGH GRADE SIX
ACTIVITY FOUR

NAME POETRY

Students will write a poem using the letters of their name as the first letter of the first word in each line of the poem.

1. Explain that in free verse poetry, a poem does not have to have rhythm or have rhyming lines.

2. Give an example of a name poem on the board.

Candy makes me
Happy.
Red M & M'S
In my
Stomach taste great!

3. For a variation of this activity have the students draw pictures to illustrate their poems.

4. Allow the students to share their poetry with the rest of the class on a volunteer basis.

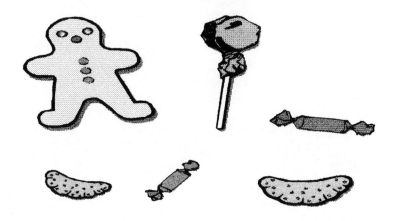

CREATE A MENU

1. Divide students into groups of four or five.

2. Each group will design a menu for a fictitious restaurant. Suggest a humorous theme.

3. The menu can be an adult or a children's menu. Each menu must include the following: a cover designed with the name of the restaurant; breakfast, lunch and dinner offerings; descriptions of offerings; prices and pictures of food. (They can use magazine cut-outs for the food).

4. When the students have finished their menus, they can share them with the rest of the class.

POLLY'S

PIZZA

PALACE

BREAKFAST
EARLY BIRD PIZZA 2.00
  Pizza covered with
  bacon, eggs, green
  peppers and onion
A.M. DELIGHT 2.50
  Pizza covered with
  sausage and cheese.
MORNING SUB 3.00
  Bacon, eggs and
  cheese on a roll

ELEMENTARY - GRADE FOUR THROUGH GRADE SIX
ACTIVITY SIX

CRYPTO PUZZLES - SOLUTIONS

The template and directions for completing these two crypto puzzles are on the following page.

Note: If the students need a hint, you can give them the letter hints listed below the solutions.

<u>SWIMMING</u>

SWIMMING IS GOOD FOR YOUR HEALTH. NO OTHER EXERCISE MAKES USE OF SO MANY MUSCLES OF THE BODY. MORE PEOPLE TAKE PART IN SWIMMING AS A FORM OF RECREATION THAN IN ANY OTHER SPORT.

HINT: W=A   C=E   X=I

<u>SAILING</u>

THE SPORT OF SAILING, IS CALLED YACHTING AND INCLUDES RACING AND ALL KINDS OF CRUISING. BEFORE THE AGE OF STEAM, SAILING VESSELS WERE THE CHIEF MEANS OF WATER TRANSPORTATION.

HINT: K=A   G=E   D=I

CRYPTO PUZZLES

Each of the messages below is written in crypto-code. One letter of the alphabet is substituted for another letter throughout the message. The phrase SAMMY IS A SMART STUDENT could be turned into the crypto DIWWU FD I DWIBH DHLZQGH, where D is substituted for S, I for A, W for M, U for Y and so on. The crytpo code is different for each puzzle.

BSXIIXRD

BSXIIXRD XB DJJV QJL UJTL FCWPOF. RJ JOFCL

CHCLNXBC IWECB TBC JQ BJ IWRU ITBNPCB JQ OFC MJVU. IJLC KCJKPC

OWEC KWLO XR BSXIIXRD WB W QJLI JQ LCNLCWOXJR OFWR XR WRU

JOFCL BKJLO.

YKDJDST

QLG YVNUQ NO YKDJDST, DY WKJJGH AKWLQDST KSH

DSWJZHGY UKWDST KSH KJJ PDSHY NO WUZDYDST. EGONUG QLG KTG
NO

YQGKR, YKDJDST BGYYGJY XGUG QLG WLGDO RGKSY NO XKQGU

QUKSYVNUQKQDNS.

MULTIPLICATION PROBLEMS

NAME _____   DATE _____

**MULTIPLY EACH SET OF
NUMBERS AND WRITE THE
ANSWER UNDER THE LINE**

8	3	6	1	2	7
x4	x4	x7	x4	x4	x4

7	9	4	5	5	1
x9	x7	x3	x5	x6	x5

9	3	8	4	9	9
x8	x9	x7	x1	x1	x6

6	4	3	4	9	7
x7	x5	x8	x1	x8	x4

8	7	5	8	5	9
x8	x7	x5	x6	x9	x3

3	7	1	4	7	5
x5	x3	x7	x6	x7	x7

SIMILES - "COOL AS A CUCUMBER"

NAME _____   **DATE** _____

A SIMILE IS A FIGURE OF SPEECH COMPARING ONE THING TO ANOTHER THAT IS VERY DIFFERENT FROM IT. a SIMILE IS INTRODUCED WITH THE WORD "LIKE" OR THE WORD "AS".

FILL IN THE BLANKS WITH SIMILES OF YOUR OWN. TRY TO MAKE YOUR COMPARISONS UNUSUAL AND COLORFUL.

It was the first day of school and I was as scared as _____.

The school looked like _____. I went into my classroom

and I saw a lot of new kids in the room. The kids were as silly as _____

_____. The teacher was standing at the blackboard. She was

writing a lesson on the board. I sat down at my desk and felt like _____

_____. The top of my desk was as clean as _____

_____. I wondered how long it would stay that way. The

classroom smelled like _____. The teacher began to talk

to us. Her voice was as soft as _____. I could hardly hear

what she was saying. The boy next to me started to laugh. His laugh was like _____

_____. The teacher started to laugh, too. Then the whole

class started to laugh. It was like _____. I think I am going to

like this class.

ELEMENTARY - GRADE FOUR THROUGH GRADE SIX
ACTIVITY NINE

CREATE A VALENTINE CARD

1. Give each student a sheet of paper that is folded into four squares. (Use the template on bottom of page.)

2. Draw the following diagrams on the board to show students how the card will look before and after it is folded. Also show them a hand-held example.

3. Have the students print "Be My Valentine" and draw a design on Box #1 (cover).

4. Students can write their own greeting on Box #3 (inside right). Write a suggested greeting on the front board.

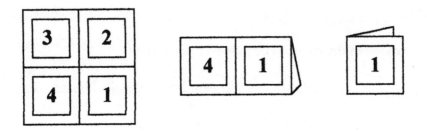

MY SUMMER VACATION

NAME _____   DATE _____

WRITE A STORY ABOUT WHAT YOU DID DURING SUMMER VACATION.

Summer Vacation

_____

_____

_____

_____

_____

_____

_____

_____

_____

THE END

MY BEST FRIEND

NAME _____   DATE _____

DRAW A PICTURE OF YOUR BEST FRIEND IN THE BOX.   THEN ANSWER THE QUESTIONS.

1. What is your best friend's name?   _____

2. How did you meet your best friend?   _____

3. How long have you been best friends?   _____

4. What does your best friend like to eat? _____

5. What kind of music does your best friend like? _____

6. What do you like best about your best friend? _____

7. What do you and your best friend do for fun? _____

DEAR DIARY

NAME _____   DATE _____

A diary or a journal entry is a short piece of writing about something that happened to you on a particular day.

Imagine that you are a famous actor or actress, and you have just finished filming a movie. Write a sample page of your diary. Give details about what happened during the day and how you feel now that the movie is finished.

Date _____

Dear Diary:

_____

_____

_____

_____

_____

_____

_____

_____

_____

_____

THE END

ONE PICTURE IS WORTH A THOUSAND WORDS

NAME _____   **DATE** _____

Draw a picture of your favorite place to visit.	Draw a picture of your least favorite food.

Write three sentences about this place.

_____

_____

_____

_____

_____

_____

_____

Write three sentences about this food.

_____

_____

_____

_____

_____

_____

_____

THINK AND SHARE

1. Students will work in pairs.

2. Each pair of students should have one sheet of paper and a pen/pencil.

3. Draw a small dot on the board. Ask the students to make a list of all the different things that the dot could be. Give them some examples:

      A BABY FLY
      A BIRD'S EYE
      A LITTLE STAR
      A SMALL STONE
      A FLEA
      A BABY EGG
      A SPECK OF DUST
      A DIAMOND
      THE HEAD OF A PIN
      A TINY FLOWER
      A PIECE OF GUM
      A CRUMB
      A HOLE
      A GRAIN OF SAND
      A SEED

4. After fifteen minutes, ask for a volunteer to write suggestions on the board.

5. Keep going around the room from one pair of students to the next, soliciting answers. Duplicate answers cannot be used, but "close" answers are acceptable.
Example:

      Acceptable: First: A piece of gum
                       Second: A piece of candy

    Not Acceptable: First: A small stone
                       Second: A pebble

ELEMENTARY - GRADE FOUR THROUGH GRADE SIX
ACTIVITY FIFTEEN

"MY FAVORITE THINGS" BINGO

1. Have each student fill in his or her personal answer in each of the bingo squares.

2. After the bingo cards are complete, make students aware of the rules of "My Favorite Things" bingo. You can tell them the rules and/or you can write the rules on the board.

<u>Rules</u>
1. You should go around the room and find another student who shares one of your favorite things.
2. You should have that student sign the square on your bingo card.
3. You cannot have the same student sign your card more than two times.
4. A student can sign squares on another student's bingo card, even if the student has already signed that square on another card.
5. The first person to get a cover-all is the winner.

My favorite color is	My favorite TV show is	My favorite season is	My favorite movie is
_____	_____	_____	_____
My birthday month is	My favorite sport is	My favorite singer is	My favorite kind of pizza is
_____	_____	_____	_____
My favorite flavor of ice cream is	My favorite candy bar is	My favorite subject in school is	My favorite movie actor is
_____	_____	_____	_____
My phone number starts with the number	The color of my toothbrush is	I go to bed around	I get up around
_____	_____	_____	_____

ELEMENTARY - GRADE FOUR THROUGH GRADE SIX
ACTIVITY SIXTEEN

ON SAFARI

1. Students will work in pairs.

2. Each student should have his or her own sheet of paper.

3. Tell students to imagine that they are going on an African Safari. One of the students is the newspaper writer and the other is the newspaper photographer.

4. Each pair should be assigned a different part of the jungle. Some areas you could suggest for the safari are:

> The monkey jungle
> The lion jungle
> The snake jungle
> The elephant jungle
> The giraffe jungle
> The leopard jungle
> The wild bird jungle
> The wild flower jungle
> The rain forest jungle

4. The newspaper writer has to write down everything they see on their safari.

5. The newspaper photographer has to take pictures (draw) while they are on safari.

6. When the students have completed their assignments, they can post the news articles and "photographs" around the room in a gallery fashion. The entire class can then walk around the gallery and view each other's work.

ELEMENTARY - GRADE FOUR THROUGH GRADE SIX
ACTIVITY SEVENTEEN

WRITING A BIOGRAPHY

1. Students will work in pairs.

2. One student in each pair should have a sheet of paper.

3. Tell students to imagine that one student is a famous author who has been hired to write the life story of a famous person from history. (the other student)

4. In each pair there should be a different historical character. Some characters from history you could suggest for the assignment are:

Neil Armstrong
Amelia Earhart
Thomas Edison
Albert Einstein
Benjamin Franklin
Martin Luther King
Abraham Lincoln
Charles Lindbergh
Rosa Parks
Eleanor Roosevelt
Betty Ross
Harriet Beecher Stone
King Tut
Mark Twain
George Washington

5. The "author" will take notes while the "famous person" tells everything their can about their life.

6. When the students have completed their assignments, they can take turns introducing their famous partners to the rest of the class.

ELEMENTARY - GRADE FOUR THROUGH GRADE SIX
ACTIVITY EIGHTEEN

WRITING AN ADVERTISEMENT

1. Students will work in groups of four or five.
2. Each group of students must design an ad for a fundraising event.
3. Have students choose where the proceeds from their fundraiser will go–band uniforms, CARE, library books, etc.
4. Tell students to imagine that they must create a poster advertisement to promote an event at their school. The poster must be designed in such a way so that it will convince students, teachers and parents to attend the fundraising event.
5. Advertisements should include information such as when the event will take place, where it will take place, cost of the tickets, etc.
6. Each group should create an advertisement for a different type of fundraiser. Some fundraisers you could suggest for the assignment are:

> A Valentine Dance
> A Sock Hop
> A Teacher / Student Basketball Game
> A Book Fair
> A Flea Market
> A Plant Sale
> A White Elephant Sale
> A School Play
> A Pep Rally
> A Spring Concert

Note: Perhaps you could bring in extra paper for the posters such as primary newsprint.

7. When the students have completed the assignment, they can share their posters with the rest of the class.

FREE-WRITING

NAME _____   **DATE** _____

      Free-writing is writing down everything that comes to mind, without stopping to think about grammar, spelling or even making sense. It is writing down all your thoughts for ten minutes without stopping to think about what you are writing.

Read the following example of free-writing:
I want to see the movie about the dinosaurs, but if I go to see that...I smell popcorn. Too bad it's so expensive. I want to see the new Disney movie. Yeah, I think I'll see that. Is that Devin over there? I wonder if I'll see Becky tonight. I think I have to baby sit for my sister. I want some popcorn. I don't care how much it costs. I think I'll see the dinosaur movie today. I'll see the Disney movie another time...or maybe I'll just wait til it's a rental. I want to rent a movie tonight if I'm going to be baby sitting for my sister. I'd better tell my mom to get some cookies, I think we're out.

Directions: Imagine that you are at a toy store. You have just been given a one-hundred dollar gift certificate. You only have fifteen minutes to decide what you will spend it on. Free-write about what you are thinking as you run through the store. Write continually for ten minutes. Do not stop to think about or edit your work.

_____

_____

_____

_____

_____

_____

_____

**ELEMENTARY - GRADE FOUR THROUGH GRADE SIX
ACTIVITY TWENTY**

MAP MAKER

1. Students will work in groups of four or five.

2. Each group of students must create a map.

3. Tell students to imagine that they must create a map to help a new student find their way from the bus drop off to the classroom, from the classroom to the playground, from the playground to the cafeteria, from the cafeteria to the media center, from the media center to the office, and from the office back to the room.

Variations:

- Students can create a legend for their map
- Students can add a compass to their map
- Students can add artwork to their map
- Students can color their map
- Students can make a scale for their map, i.e. one inch equals ten feet

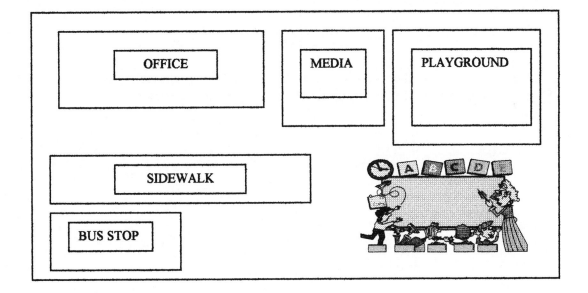

MIDDLE SCHOOL
ACTIVITY ONE

THINK AND SHARE

1. Students will work in pairs.

2. Each pair of students should have one sheet of paper and a pen/pencil.

3. Ask students to spend fifteen minutes building a list of all the different ways they can use a brick. Give them some examples:

> PAPERWEIGHT
> DOOR STOP
> WEAPON
> DINNER PLATE
> BOOK END
> TABLE LEG
> BAKING STONE
> GRILL CLEANER
> MUSICAL INSTRUMENT
> FLY SWATTER

4. After fifteen minutes, ask for a volunteer to write suggestions on the board.

5. Keep going around the room from one pair of students to the next, soliciting answers.
Duplicate answers cannot be used, but "close" answers are acceptable.
Example:

> Acceptable: FIRST: FLY SWATTER
> SECOND: TOOL FOR EXTERMINATORS

> Not Acceptable: FIRST: PAPER WEIGHT
> SECOND: SOMETHING TO HOLD DOWN PAPER

**MIDDLE SCHOOL
ACTIVITY TWO**

COOPERATIVE WRITING - UFO STORY

1. Divide students into groups of five.

2. Tell the students that they will be writing a story about a UFO sighting. Put the first sentence of the story on the board.

    One morning, when I was waiting for the school bus, I saw something very strange.

3. The UFO story is passed around the group and each student adds a new sentence. Note: Sometimes it is fun to fold the paper so you can't see what the others have written when you write your sentence.

4. The UFO story must "circle" the group at least two times (ten sentences).

5. Have the group edit the finished story. If they want, the students can draw a UFO, cut it out of construction paper and attach their story to the front. These UFO's can be hung on the walls or suspended from the ceiling.

6. Have each student sign the group story.

7. Have students share their stories with the rest of the class.

**MIDDLE SCHOOL
ACTIVITY THREE**

STORY TELLING

1. Write the following story introduction on the board or make and distribute a copy of the introduction to each student.

> Today is the first time Jason and Bill have ever taken a shortcut home from school. Jason thinks they can get home at least ten minutes earlier than usual if they go by the old Spooner mansion. But today it will take Jason and Bill a long, long time to get home. In fact, they will be lucky to get home at all!

2. Circling the room in one direction, each student in the class will add a new sentence to the story.

3. Students keep adding sentences to the story until everyone has had a chance.

4. Ask for volunteers to suggest the final sentence or two of the story.

5. The students will receive a group grade on the project.

Note: You might ask one or two students to write the story down as it is being developed (told) by the class members.

MIDDLE SCHOOL
ACTIVITY FOUR

GHOSTLY SCAVENGER HUNT

Note: You will need permission to bring students to the media center in order to complete this activity.

1. Students can choose to work alone or with a partner. If working in pairs, both students must complete a paper.

2. Write the following questions on the board and have students copy the list.

3. Students must find the answers to the questions using books they find in the media center. They must write the answer to the question, the name of the book where they found the answer and also the page number from the book. Students must not share answers with anyone but their partner.

4. Students will have different answers to many of the questions. This is acceptable.

GHOSTLY QUESTIONS

1. Write the definition of Halloween.

2. Halloween is in October. Name another holiday in October.

3. <u>The Headless Horseman</u> is a scary story. Who wrote it?

4. Find the name of another story that would be good for Halloween.

5. Halloween is a "scary" holiday. List five other adjectives for the word scary.

6. Find an article in the newspaper or in a magazine that is scary.

7. <u>A woman wrote Frankenstein</u>. What is her name?

8. What is the average temperature in New York City on Halloween day?

9. What is a "goblin"?

10. What is a "phantom"?

**MIDDLE SCHOOL
ACTIVITY FIVE**

HAIKU POETRY

1. Write the definition of Haiku poetry on the board:

> Haiku - a type of Japanese poetry that depicts a scene from nature. The first line is five syllables, the second line is seven syllables and the third line is five syllables.

Example:

> ### Trees have many leaves
> ### With colors bright and lovely
> ### That soon will fall off.

2. Ask students to write an original Haiku and then draw a picture that illustrates their poetry. If crayons and markers are available, allow the students to use them in their drawings.

3. If time permits, allow students to share their poetry with the entire class.

MIDDLE SCHOOL
ACTIVITY SIX

CREATIVE DRAMA

1. Divide students into groups of four or five students

2. Each group will develop a skit from a well-known fairy tale. Some suggestions are:

> Little Red Riding Hood
> The Three Little Pigs
> Hansel and Gretel
> Rumpelstiltskin
> Snow White
> Sleeping Beauty
> Cinderella
> Beauty and the Beast
> The Emperor's New Clothes
> The Elves and The Shoemaker
> Thumbelina
> Jack and the Beanstalk

The skit will be performed completely in mime (no dialogue), in front of the rest of the class. Allow students fifteen minutes preparation time.

3. Encourage students to create props for their skits.

4. The audience must not guess which fairy tale is being presented until the skit is completed. Once the skit is over, the audience will try to guess the fairy tale and they should also identify each of the characters.

5. The process is repeated until all the groups have presented their skits.

Note: If it is at all possible, arrange for the skits to be video-taped. The videos can then be played for the classroom teacher upon his/her return. The videos can also be shown in other classes.

MIDDLE SCHOOL
ACTIVITY SEVEN

COOPERATIVE LEARNING

Note: This activity can be used with any type of reading material. Some examples of reading materials to use are: textbooks, scholastic magazines or a copy of the daily newspaper.

1. Have students divide into groups of four or five.

2. The assignment should be equally divided between groups. Each group must work on a different reading assignment. Each group will read and become "experts" on one section of the reading assignment.

3. After reading the assignment, each group will present a summary of their section to the rest of the class.

4. Each group should have one paper that has on it, the names of each group member and the page(s) of the reading assignment. Also, the group must compose two questions that pertain to the information they present. The questions can be used for a class quiz. The students will receive a group grade for the assignment.

5. If time allows, collect the assignment sheet from each group and give a quiz to the class using the questions that each group has prepared. In this instance, the students will receive two grades for the activity; one for the group work and one for the quiz.

MIDDLE SCHOOL
ACTIVITY EIGHT

MEDIA IN THE CLASSROOM

1. Divide the students into groups of four or five.

2. Ask the students if they know what PSA (Public Service Announcements) are and ask if someone can give an example of a current PSA running on television or radio. Some examples might be:

> Big Brother or Big Sister Commercial
> Adult Literacy Program - Teach a Friend to Read Commercial
> Boy Scouts of America Commercial
> Girl Scouts of America Commercial
> Smoky the Bear - How to Prevent Forest Fires Commercial
> American Heart Foundation - Stop Smoking Commercial

3. Students will then create their own 60 second PSA to be presented to the rest of the class.

4. Provide students with the following guidelines:

> Choose a charity or non profit group to represent
> Choose media source - television or radio
> Create a powerful introductory phrase, such as
> > "Did you know that forest fires kill one million wild animals every year?"
> Students will have fifteen minutes to create and rehearse commercial.

5. Encourage students to create props for their commercials.

5. Groups will take turns presenting their commercials to the rest of the class.

6. Class audience should discuss whether or not each PSA is effective and state the reasons for their opinions.

Note: If it is at all possible, arrange for the commercials to be video-taped. The videos can then be played for the classroom teacher upon his/her return. The videos can also be shown in other classes.

MIDDLE SCHOOL
ACTIVITY NINE

CATEGORIES

Note: Students can work alone or in pairs

1. Students will fill in the category grid template on the next page.

2. Students cannot use the dictionary for the first ten minutes of the activity.

3. After all the students have completed the grid, ask for a volunteer to write students' answers on the board. Students will then take turns giving answers until all the responses that the students used on their personal grids are listed on the board.

Below is an example of the completed category grid. There are no right or wrong answers. All answers are acceptable as long as they begin with the correct letter and fall into the correct category.

	ANIMAL	BIRD	CITY	PROFESSION	FOOD
S	Sheep	Sparrow	St. Lewis	Surgeon	Shrimp
C	Cat	Crow	Cincinnati	Carpenter	Cucumber
O	Orangutan	Ostrich	Orlando	Orthodontist	Onion
R	Rabbit	Robin	Richmond	Repairman	Rice
E	Elephant	Eagle	El Paso	Electrician	Egg

Variation: You can create your own categories for the grids. Be certain to complete your grid before you ask students to do so because it is sometimes very difficult to find answers for all the grid categories. If it takes you longer than two minutes to think of a response, then the grid category/letter is probably too complex for a middle student to complete; find an alternate category/letter.

NAME _____   DATE _____

CATEGORIES

	ANIMAL	BIRD	CITY	PROFESSION	FOOD
S					
C					
O					
R					
E					

**MIDDLE SCHOOL
ACTIVITY TEN**

HOW-TO PRESENTATION

1. On a sheet of paper, have students write an outline for a two-minute speech on "How-to" do something. You can present the following ideas to the students as suggestions for speech topics:

How to eat an Oreo
How to tie your shoes
How to fly a kite
How to ride a bike
How to wash your face
How to make a peanut butter and jelly sandwich
How to wrap a present
How to give your dog a bath
How to clean your room
How to play hop scotch
How to jump rope
How to bake a cake
How to make a paper airplane
How to ride a skateboard
How to roller skate
How to build a fire
How to ride a horse
How to take a picture
How to braid your hair

2. After writing their outlines, students should get into groups of four or five students.

3. Students will present their "How-to" speech to the other members in their group.

4. After everyone has given a speech to their groups members, the best "How-to" speech from each group can be presented to the entire class.

5. Students will turn in their speech outlines for grading purposes.

NAME STORY

1. Students will write a story where each sentence begins with a letter from their name.

2. The first letter of each sentence should be in bold type (or darker ink) so that their name stands out when you look at the story.

3. The teacher may ask that students use middle names, so that the story is a bit longer.

4. Read the following example to the students. Tell them the name of the author and emphasize each letter in the student's name as you read it aloud.

Carmela Marotta

Candy is my favorite food. **A**nytime I am hungry, I reach for candy. **R**aisins covered with chocolate are always a special treat. **M** and M's are good to eat when I'm at school. **E**very time I eat candy, I smile.   **L**ollipops are great, because they last a long time. **A** jawbreaker lollipop sometimes lasts an hour.

My favorite candy of all time is chocolate. **A** chocolate bar first thing in the morning, gives me energy. **R**eeses Pieces are good, because they are chocolate and peanut butter mixed together. **O**'Henry bars are good because they have chocolate and nuts. **T**he very best chocolate candy bar in the world is a Milky Way Bar. **T**hey have chocolate and caramel mixed together. **A**ll in all, I'd say, I'm a candy nut!

**MIDDLE SCHOOL
ACTIVITY TWELVE**

PERSONALITY POEM

1. To begin this assignment, students can draw either a silhouette of themselves or a paper doll type of body.

2. Next, students will write a ten line poem about themselves. They will write two sentences for each of the following categories:

Note: List categories on blackboard

> Physical description
> Way he/she talks
> Sound of his/her voice
> Interests/hobbies
> Something special about him/her

You could put the following example on the front board:

> I wish I wasn't quite so short.
> I wish I had blond hair.
> I wish my voice was very deep,
> I wish my brain was rare.
> But I'm not tall and my hair's brown,
> And my voice is kind of high.
> And as for brains, I'm no Einstein,
> I'm just an average kind of guy.
> There is something I do quite well
> I make kids laugh with the stories I tell.

MIDDLE SCHOOL
ACTIVITY THIRTEEN

CREATIVE DRAMA - THE "REAL" STORY

One of the suggested reading books in Chapter Four is *The True Story of the 3 Little Pigs,* written by Jon Scieszka. This story parodies (pokes fun at) the story of the 3 little pigs. In this book, the wolf is the good guy.

1. If you have this book, begin the activity by reading the story. If you do not have the book, explain a parody. You can use movie examples such as:

Robin Hood - Men in Tights	For	*Robin Hood*
Ten Things I Hate About You	For	*Taming of the Shrew*
Clueless	For	*Emma*
Young Frankenstein	For	*Frankenstein*

2. Divide the class into groups of four or five students each.

3. Have each group write a script for a short skit, which parodies a favorite fairy tale. Some examples of fairy tales they might parody are:

Little Red Riding Hood
The Three Little Pigs
Hansel and Gretel
Rumpelstiltskin
Snow White
Sleeping Beauty
Cinderella
Beauty and the Beast
The Emperor's New Clothes
The Elves and The Shoemaker
Thumbelina
Jack and the Beanstalk

4. Allow the students fifteen minutes to write their scripts and rehearse their skits.

5. Have each group perform their skit for the rest of the class.

Note: If it is at all possible, arrange for the skits to be video-taped. The videos can then be played for the classroom teacher upon his/her return. The videos can also be shown in other classes.

MIDDLE SCHOOL
ACTIVITY FOURTEEN

LETTER TO FAVORITE TEACHER

1. Ask students to think about their favorite teacher. What makes that teacher special? What did he or she learn from that teacher?

2. Ask each student to write a letter to that teacher telling the teacher why he or she is such a special teacher.

3. Offer the following suggestions as to the topics that the students may want to write about:

> Favorite lesson
> Favorite project
> Favorite book
> Favorite field trip
> Favorite time of the day
> Favorite time of the year
> The teacher's personality
> The classroom atmosphere

4. Working in pairs, have the students edit their partner's letters.

5. Have students re-write the letters and if possible, find the addresses/schools of the teachers and send the actual letters. The students will be pleasantly surprised with the responses they will receive.

Note: An alternative for this assignment would be to write a special "thank you for being you" letter, to a special relative or friend.

MIDDLE SCHOOL
ACTIVITY FIFTEEN

COMPUTER DETECTIVE

Note: While it is possible to do this activity in the classroom, it is designed to be carried out in a writing/computer lab.

1. Have each student bring a book of some type to the computer lab.

2. The student is to type a paragraph from the book, word for word, into the computer, and "SAVE". Then, the student will change one sentence completely and "SAVE".

3. The students will then move to different computers, read the paragraph on the monitor and put a response at the bottom of the screen, noting which sentence he/she believes to be changed.

4. This process is repeated three times. The students are then asked to return to their original computer to check the responses.

5. Ask the class if any students were able to completely stump their fellow students. If so, have these students type the correct sentence below their paragraph and "PRINT". You can take these "stumpers" back to the classroom and use for extra credit assignments at a future date.

6. If time permits, you can repeat this activity.

MIDDLE SCHOOL
ACTIVITY SIXTEEN

FOLLOW THE LEADER

1. Have the students sit in a circle in the center of the room.

2. One student leaves the room.

3. One student from the circle is chosen as the leader. Whatever action the leader makes, the rest of the circle will mimic. The idea is to have everyone doing the same thing at the same time. The students will want to make it very difficult for the incoming student to decide who the leader is.

Offer the following suggestions as to actions that the students might perform:

> Hands on head
> Cross legs
> Clap hands
> Stand on one leg
> Hop
> Kneel down
> Turn around
> Touch their toes
> Shake hands with a neighbor
> Put hands on waist

4. The student returns to the room and joins the circle. The action begins.

5. The returning student has to guess which student is the leader.

6. When he/she guesses correctly, the old leader leaves the room, a new leader is chosen and the activity continues.

MIDDLE SCHOOL
ACTIVITY SEVENTEEN

CREATING CLUSTERS

1. Give students the following definition of "clustering".

      Clustering is when you bubble the topic you want to write about. Next, you think of ideas that go along with your topic and you connect these ideas to your topic bubble with more bubbles. These new bubbles can lead to other bubbles in the same way.

2. Draw the following clustering example on the board or on an overhead transparency.

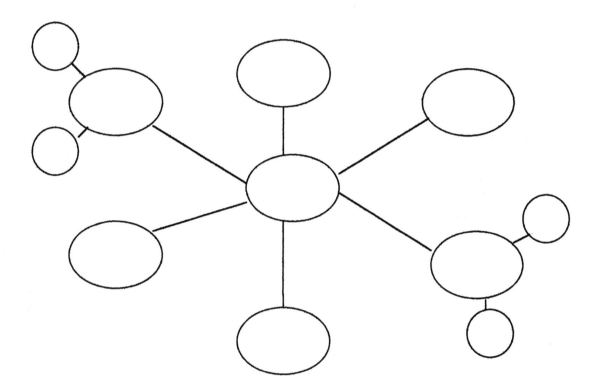

3. Have students choose a topic and complete a cluster.

MIDDLE SCHOOL
ACTIVITY EIGHTEEN

TOPIC SENTENCES

1. Give students the following definition of a topic sentence.
   The topic sentence is the most important sentence in a paragraph. It tells the reader what the paragraph is going to be about.

2. Put the following list on the board or on an overhead transparency. Tell the students they need to make a topic sentence for each of the listed subjects.

   Example: The fear of heights

   People are afraid of many different things, one such fear is the fear of heights.

Make each of the following subjects into a topic sentence.

   Violence in Video Games
   Babies Using Computers
   The Kind of Music Teens Like
   Latch-Key Children
   Neighborhood Crime
   Homework for Teenagers
   College Scholarships for Athletes
   Mass Transportation
   The Value of A College Education
   School Dress Codes

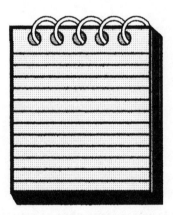

**MIDDLE SCHOOL
ACTIVITY NINETEEN**

MY HERO

1. Ask students to think about their hero. What makes that person special? What is it about the hero that makes the student want to try to be like his or her hero?

2. Ask each student to write a letter to that hero telling the hero why he or she is so special.

3. Offer the following heroes as suggested heroes whom the students may want to write about:

       MOVIE STAR
       ACTRESS OR ACTOR
       MUSICIAN
       TEACHER
       FAMILY DOCTOR
       POLITICIAN
       FRIEND
       PARENT
       GRANDPARENT
       BROTHER
       SISTER
       INVENTOR
       ATHLETE
       WRITER

4. Working in pairs, have the students edit their partner's letters.

5. Have students re-write the letters and if possible, find the addresses of the heroes and send the actual letters. The students will be pleasantly surprised with the responses they will receive.

**MIDDLE SCHOOL
ACTIVITY TWENTY**

NOUN PURSUIT

1. Give students the following definition of a noun:
    A noun is the name of a person, place, thing, or idea. All nouns are either proper nouns or common nouns. A proper noun is the name of a particular person, place, or thing and is spelled with a capital letter. A common noun is the name of a class of persons, places, things, or ideas and is not capitalized.

2. Have each student take out a book. It can be a book from the classroom, a book from another subject, a library book, a novel, a newspaper or a magazine.

3. Tell the students that that have fifteen minutes to list every noun that they can find in the book. If it is a proper noun, capitalize the noun.

4. When time is up, find out who has the most nouns in the classroom. If you have small prizes with you, you might want to give a prize to the top two or three students.

5. Ask the students to choose ten of the nouns they found and write a short poem. You can offer them the following example:

THESE ARE THE NOUNS I FOUND:

NEPHEW	BOOK	TOM	NEWSPAPER	MALL
DREAM	DOLLAR	CHANGE	ICE CREAM	DOG

THIS IS THE POEM I WROTE:

I WENT TO THE MALL WITH MY **NEPHEW TOM**.
HE WANTED TO BUY A **BOOK**.
HE GOT SOME MONEY FROM HIS MOM
A **DOLLAR** WAS ALL HE TOOK.

I TOLD TOM HE MUST BE IN A **DREAM**
LOOKING FOR A BOOK FOR A **DOLLAR**
A DOLLAR WON'T EVEN BUY **ICE CREAM**
A DOLLAR WON'T BUY A **DOG** COLLAR.

TOM SAID, ""I AM NOT DREAMING AND I AM NOT STRANGE"
"I WANT A TWENTY-FIVE CENT **NEWSPAPER**, AND **CHANGE**."

**HIGH SCHOOL
ACTIVITY ONE**

MEDIA IN THE CLASSROOM

1. Have students form groups of four or five students.

2. Students will create a sixty-second television commercial. They must decide what they want to sell, how they plan to market the product and the message they want to convey to the audience. Allow students fifteen minutes to create and rehearse the commercial.

3. Some products you might suggest that they sell are:

SHAVING CREAM
CANDY CANES
VITAMINS
BANANAS
BIRTHDAY CAKES
FLOWERS
AUTOMOBILES
PIZZA
DISH DETERGENT
LAUNDRY DETERGENT
BREAKFAST CEREAL
HAIR SHAMPOO

3. Groups will take turns presenting commercials to the rest of the class.

4. After each commercial is presented, have the class discuss the effectiveness of the commercial with one another. Would they buy the product? Why or why not?

5. Repeat the process until all the groups have presented their commercials and all the commercials have been analyzed in class discussion.

HIGH SCHOOL
ACTIVITY TWO

CREATIVE DRAMA IMPROVISATIONAL SKITS

Explain to the students that one person will begin the skit and whenever another student feels as though he/she can join in the skit, the student should just join in. After a few lines another student should join in and then after a few lines the fourth student will join the skit. The skit can continue with all four participants for a couple of minutes and then someone should say something to end the skit. The best way to introduce this activity is to be an active performer in the first skit. Ask for three students to volunteer to act in the first skit. Perform the following skit with three student volunteers. Give the three volunteers a minute or two to look over the example skit.

Example:

Teacher:	*Standing in elevator — presses imaginary floor button, says,* "I have to go all the way to the twelfth floor. I hope no one else gets on this elevator". *Pretends that elevator stops. Looks annoyed.*
1st Student:	*Enters elevator.* Says, "Could you press ten for me? I never thought the elevator would get here. I've been waiting for five minutes. Oh, I made a mistake. Could you press twelve for me?"
2nd Student:	*Enters elevator. Pretends that he/she cannot speak English. Is trying to get directions to the dentist's office.*
3rd Student:	*Enters elevator. Is wearing a Walkman and dancing to the music. Presses floor button and then starts singing to the music very loudly.*
End of Skit	All four people get to the twelfth floor and get out of the elevator.

Since this is improvisational, ask for one student to start the next skit. The fourth student up, stops the skit. Continue until all students have performed in at least one skit.

HIGH SCHOOL
ACTIVITY THREE

INTERNAL MONOLOGUE

1. Offer the following definition of a monologue to students:
    A monologue is a dramatic scene or a literary composition (such as a poem) which is performed by one person. It can also be a long speech monopolizing a conversation. An internal monologue is a monologue that goes on in your mind.

2. Tell the students that the assignment is to write an internal monologue. They will free-write, write without stopping for ten minutes about what is going on in their head during a given situation.

3. Offer up the following example:

    THIS IS AN INTERNAL MONOLOGUE FOR A PERSON WHO IS SECOND IN LINE AT A FAST FOOD RESTAURANT.

    What am I going to have today? I guess I could get a hamburger, but last time I got a hamburger here, I got sick. I really should get a salad, I need to lose weight. What is that chef doing in the back? I think he just took a bun out of the trash and put it up on the grill! Yuck!. No hamburger for me today. I guess it's a salad. I really should start working out at the gym. What is that kid doing? He just put about a hundred ketchup packets on his tray! Where is his mother, anyway? I had better order some low fat dressing. No use getting a salad if I'm going to pig out on the good stuff. And, I'd better order a diet soda, too. What? What do I want? I'll have two cheeseburgers, an order of fries, and a milk shake. And, get me lots of ketchup.

4. Tell the students that for their internal monologue, they should pretend to be second in line at the concession stand at the movies.

5. When the students have finished writing their internal monologues, ask for volunteers to read their monologues to the rest of the class.

**HIGH SCHOOL
ACTIVITY FOUR**

STORY TELLING - TALL TALES

1. Divide the class into groups of four or five students.

2. Each student will tell his/her group members a two or three minute story. It might be true or it might be completely make believe.

Offer the following examples:

"My mother and father met when they were both serving in the Army."
"I traveled to twelve states and two countries before I was five years old."
"I have a collection of two-thousand baseball cards."
"Last year I read twenty-two books."
"I like to eat peanut butter and banana sandwiches."

3. When the student is finished telling the story, the rest of the group will decide if the story was true or make believe.

4. The process continues until all the students have told a five minute story to their group members.

5. The most believable story from each group should be told to the entire class and put to a vote as to whether it is true or make believe.

6. It is great to have a prize or two—a book or a pencil or pen—for the "best" story tellers.

CREATE A LIMERICK

1. Offer the following definition of a Limerick to the students:

    A Limerick is a humorous poem of five lines. The first, second and fifth lines rhyme and have three stressed syllables. The third and fourth lines rhyme and have two stressed syllables.

2. Read the following example of a limerick to the class:

> There once was a lady from Orlando.
> She lived her whole life in a piano.
> She played a sad tune.
> In the month of June.
> When in a sinkhole her piano fell into.

3. Ask students to write an original Limerick. If time allows the students can draw a picture that illustrates their poem. If crayons and/or markers are available, allow the students to use them in their drawings.

ROUND ROBIN MEMORY GAME

1. Students should put desks/chairs in a circle.

2. Set the scene for this round robin story for the students:

> We work in a department store. Some lady was doing her Christmas shopping and had her cart filled with all sorts of items when she remembered that she left some spaghetti sauce cooking on her stove. She ran out of the store and the manager said that each of us has to take one item out of the shopping cart and return it to the correct department.

3. Each student must return an item that begins with the same letter as the first letter of his/her name.

4. Each student must say the names and items of all the students that returned items before him/her before he/she can tell what their item is.

Example:

1st student:	My name is Crystal and I returned the can opener.
2nd student:	Crystal returned the can opener. My name is Bill and I returned the buttons.
3rd student:	Crystal returned the can opener. Bill returned the buttons. My name is Tracy and I returned the towels.
4th student:	Crystal returned the can opener. Bill returned the buttons. Tracy returned the towels. My name is Stephanie and I returned the shampoo.

The game continues all around the circle. Whenever someone cannot remember a prior students' name or item returned, he/she is eliminated from the game. In the second round each student adds another item and must now recall the two items that other students have returned.

YOU ARE A FILM CRITIC

1. Students will work in pairs. Each pair will decide upon a movie to review. Each member of the pair can have the same point of view or a different view.

2. Students will have ten minutes to prepare a "thumbs up" or "thumbs down" review to present to the rest of the class. They must present concrete examples of what they liked or disliked about the movie.

3. Offer the following example of a movie review:

Lost in the Third Dimension is a must see movie for all science fiction movie buffs to see. Starring Will Loman as the spaceship captain and Fanny Hill as the alien, this movie will make the hairs on your neck stand up on end. It all begins in a ninth grade algebra class. The teacher turns her back to write on the black board and when she turns around the classroom is empty. The students have all been zapped into the third dimension. Captain Will Loman, of the starship "Quadratic", goes on a mission to find the lost class. There is breathtaking adventure during every mile of his trip. Don't wait for this one to come out on video. It's worth paying full price to see it in the theater now.

3. When students have completed the reviews, they can take turns presenting their critiques.

**HIGH SCHOOL
ACTIVITY EIGHT**

YESTERDAY AND TODAY - VENN DIAGRAM

1. Have students draw two large intersecting circles on a piece of paper.

2. Label one circle *Elementary School*, Label the second circle, *High School*, and label the middle section *All Schools*.

3. Have students list events or situations that only happen in elementary school in the first circle.

4. Have students list events or situations that only happen in high school in the second circle.

5. Have students list events or situations that only happen in all schools in the intersecting part of the diagram.

6. When students are finished, draw a large Venn Diagram on the front board and ask representatives from each group to come up and put one item in each section. Continue having students add to the diagram until all events and situations have been written on the board.

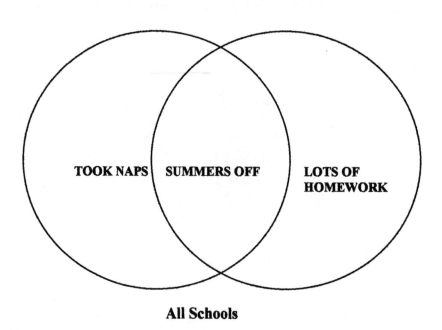

All Schools

Elementary School   **High School**

BLIND SPOTS IN AMERICA

Most people learn the names of all the states when they are in elementary school. For that reason, most high school students (and most adults) think they can easily name all the states. But the simple and disturbing fact is that the majority of people cannot name all the states. There is a definite blind spot when it comes to the Midwestern section of the country. Explain this actuality to the students and ask them to write down the names of all the states as quickly as possible. Do not be surprised if no one can complete this assignment!

To make the assignment more challenging, you can ask the students to draw their own maps from memory and then fill in the state names.

WHAT KIND OF LEARNER ARE YOU?

The following activity is designed to help students discover what type of learners they are.

A visual learner (V) learns by seeing information.
An audio learner (A) learns by listening to information.
A tactile learner (T) learns by touching information.

Note: Recreate the following drawing on the board to use as an example when explaining the directions of this activity to the students.

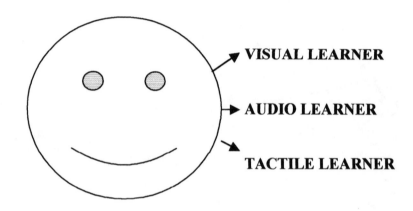

1. Students will work in pairs. Arrange desks/ chairs so that students are directly facing one another.
2. One student will use the worksheet on the following page to ask his or her partner each of the ten questions. The student asking the question must look directly into the respondent's eyes and record the first movement of the respondent's eyes, by placing an arrow on the face going in the direction of the eye movement.
3. When one student has answered all ten questions, the other student will tally up how many arrows go in each direction. Whichever direction (up, side, down) has the most arrows, suggests the student's learning style. For example: If a student has the majority of arrows going up, he or she is a visual learner. It is unusual, but possible to learn equally well in two or three areas.
4. Repeat the activity with students changing roles and using new worksheets.

STUDENT ASKING QUESTIONS: _____

STUDENT RESPONDING TO QUESTIONS: _____

1. What is the color of your living room carpet?

2. What would you look like with green hair?

3. What was your first grade teacher's name?

4. What color is your bedspread?

5. What is the color of your front door?

6. What did you have for breakfast?

7. How old is your teacher?

8. What is your middle name?

9. What is the president's name?

10. Name the five Great Lakes.

**HIGH SCHOOL
ACTIVITY ELEVEN**

FORTUNE TELLER AD-LIB

Elements of mystery will make this ad-lib activity a lot of fun.

1. Divide students into pairs.

2. Write the following interview questions on an overhead projector film or on the blackboard.

3. Have each student number a paper from one to twenty-four.

4. Using the interview questions, students will write down the answers their partners give them on their answer sheet.

5. Hand out ad-lib templates on next page. Using the answers from the interviews, the students will fill in the ad-lib worksheets. The finished products are usually quite humorous.

6. Ask for volunteers to read their completed ad-libs to the class.

Say the first thing that comes to mind when asked about the following items.

1. Snack item
2. Your name
3. Your age
4. A solid
5. A liquid
6. Something soft
7. TV show
8. A person's name
9. Talent - #1
10. Talent - #2
11. Place of business #1
12. Number between 1 & 100
13. Number between 18 and 100
14. A type of personality
15. A type of body size
16. A type of odor
17. A profession
18. A place of business - #2
19. Name of a state
20. Even number between 2 & 20
21. Inexpensive make of car
22. Heavy machinery
23. Verb ending in "ing"
24. Animal

Fortune Teller Ad-Lib

My name is 1. _____ and I am a fortune teller. I will tell you about your future. Your name is 2. _____ and you are 3. _____ years old. Your favorite food is 4. _____ and your favorite drink is 5. _____. You love to wear 6. _____, when you relax around the house. Your favorite TV show is 7. _____. Your best friend is 8. _____ because of his/her 9. _____ and 10. _____. Next summer you will get a part-time job at 11. _____.

You will have 12. _____ steadies before you meet your spouse. You will get married when you are 13. _____ years old. Your spouse will be 14. _____ and 15. _____ and 16. _____. You will work as a 17. _____ at 18. _____ in the state of 19. _____. You will have 20. _____ children; half girls and half boys.

You will drive a 21. _____ to and from work, but on weekends you'll travel by 22. _____. You will become very famous because you will write a book about 23. _____ . You will retire at age fifty-five and spend the rest of your days traveling with a 24. _____ as your companion(s).

CLASSMATE BINGO

1. Have each student tell the class his or her name and one bit of information about himself or herself. For example–My name is Billy and I like to roller blade.

2. After the introductions are complete, make students aware of the rules of "Classmate Bingo". You can tell them the rules and/or you can write the rules on the board.

<u>Rules</u>

1. Sign the middle square of your own bingo sheet
2. Go around the room and ask other students if they can sign one of your squares.
3. Other students can sign one or two squares for you, but no more than two.
4. The first person to get a cover-all is the winner.

has attended more than one school	has lived in another state	has a brother	has a sister	knows how to ride a skateboard
can play a musical instrument	owns a pair of boots	ate at McDonalds last week	owns a dog	owns a cat
has bowled at least once this year	has a part-time job	FREE SPACE	has played baseball on a team	has been to Disney World
likes to listen to music	likes to watch soap operas	knows how to play chess	likes to work-out	has attended summer school
owns at least one Barbie doll	owns a bicycle	knows how to swim	went to the mall last week	has more than one watch

HIGH SCHOOL
ACTIVITY THIRTEEN

TIC - TAC - TOE - GAME SHOW

1. Divide the class into two groups.

2. Have students in each group prepare index cards with different trivia questions and answers on the cards.   Here are some suggested trivia questions/answers:

- Name the five Great Lakes
    Answer: Lake Erie, Lake Superior, Lake Huron, Lake Michigan
              and Lake Ontario
- Name the last two states to be admitted to the United States
    Answer: Alaska and Hawaii
- Name the five vowels - do not include the letter "y"
    Answer: A, E, I, O and U
- Name the last five presidents of the United States
    Answer: Bill Clinton, George Bush, Ronald Reagan, Jimmy Carter and
              Gerald Ford
- How many "i"'s are there in Mississippi
    Answer: Four

3. Choose a game host or hostess for each side.

4. Draw a large tic-tac-toe board on the front board.

5. Have the host/hostess from one group ask a question of the other group. If they answer correctly, within the allotted time, the group gets an "X". If they answer incorrectly, or not at all, "O" gets the square.

6. Continue in this manner until one group wins the game.

**HIGH SCHOOL
ACTIVITY FOURTEEN**

FICTION FROM FACT

1. Students will write an original journalistic fiction paper based on a true story article from the local newspaper.

2. Students will develop the story by changing the names and places in the story.

3. Students will attach a copy of the original news story to the finished paper.

Note: Below are some basic guidelines on writing journalistic fiction that can be given to students before they begin this assignment:

- Write an authentic story that is individual and unique, but also representative of human experience as a whole.
- Use information that is accurate and carefully researched. This is extremely important because, with most of these stories, readers will have heard news accounts and will lose faith in the story if there are inconsistencies.
- Develop a central thesis that has grown out of the author's research.
- Create enough development to show the relationship between the characters' actions and what happens. People's motives are explored, and cause and effect are tied together.

Allow the characters to reveal themselves through their speech and actions, rather than through the author's descriptions.

SOLVE THE MYSTERY

1. Divide the class into groups of four or five students. Have two students volunteer to read the following dialogue between a man and a woman:

Man:	**Quick, shut the door and come here!**
Woman:	**What happened? Is that blood on your hands?**
Man:	**Quiet! We have to be quiet. Someone might hear us and come inside. Did you bring the box?**
Woman:	**Yes, I have the box, But, it's locked and I couldn't find a key. What's going on? Are you in trouble?**
Man:	**Wait a minute while I catch my breath and then I'll tell you everything.**

2. Ask the students to decide within their groups what the reason is for this dialogue. They will then write the end of the script.

3. When the scripts are finished, have the students take turns performing their skits in front of the class.

HIGH SCHOOL
ACTIVITY SIXTEEN

ROUND ROBIN IN THE COMPUTER LAB

Note: While it is possible to do this activity in the classroom, it is designed to be carried out in a writing/computer lab.

1. Tell students that they are going to write a story, one sentence at a time.

2. Each student should type their name at the top of the screen then scroll down and center a title for their story. Next, each student should type the opening line to their story on the computer and hit "SAVE". Some students might have a bit of difficulty coming up with an opening sentence, so you might want to make some suggestions. You can use the following examples:

> It was a dark and stormy night in the middle of November when I first met Jason.

> Jennifer was a strange sort of girl, she always kind of frightened me.

> I can remember my first day at camp as though it were yesterday, even though I was only five years old.

> It was a beautiful and windy day in March, when I flew a kite for the first time.

3. When the first sentence is typed, the students move to the computers on their left. At the new station, the students will read what had been typed so far, and add a sentence to it, and "SAVE".

4. The activity proceeds in this manner until every student has been to every computer. When the students return to their own computers, they will read the story and write a final sentence or two to end the story.

5. Print stories and bring back to room to share on another day.

Note: Because of time constraints, you may have to send students back to their original story to complete it before they have had time to completely circle the room.

HIGH SCHOOL
ACTIVITY SEVENTEEN

NEWSPAPER SCAVENGER HUNT

Note: You will have to go to the media center to complete this activity

Directions: Use a newspaper to find the answers to the following questions.

1. What is the headline story? _____

2. Who wrote the story? _____

3. What was the temperature yesterday in Las Vegas, Nevada? _____

4. Which city in the United States had the highest temperature yesterday?
    _____

4. What is the first letter to Dear Abby about? _____

5. On what page did you find the comics? _____

6. Name three movies that are playing in the theater today.

    _____

    _____

    _____

7. Which section has the most full or half-page ads on it? _____

8. On what page(s) would you find information about the stock market? _____

9. How many people are listed in the obituaries that were under the age of fifty when
    they died? _____

10. Find a story about children in the newspaper. What is the title? _____

11. Look at the advertisements in the newspaper. List three things that you would like to
    buy. _____

    _____

    _____

12. Find a political or editorial cartoon in the newspaper. What is it about?

    _____

HIGH SCHOOL
ACTIVITY EIGHTEEN

ONOMATOPOEIA

1. Offer the following definition of onomatopoeia to the students:

> Onomatopoeia is the use of words whose sounds suggest their meanings. Edgar Allan Poe uses onomatopoeia in his poem, "The Bells" [1827].

2. Read a portion of Poe's poem to the class:

> How they clang, and clash, and roar!
> What a horror they outpour
> On the bosom of the palpitating air!
> Yet the ear, it fully knows
> By the twanging
> And the clanging....

3. Ask students to write an original poem and use onomatopoeia to draw attention to sound in their poems. If time allows, the students can draw a picture that illustrates their poem. If crayons and/or markers are available, allow the students to use them in their drawings.

4. Students can volunteer to do a dramatic reading of their poems for the rest of the class.

CAMPAIGN SPEECH

1. Offer the following definition of a campaign to the students:
   When a candidate is running for office, he or she gives a campaign speech in order to tell the voters about his or her positions on various matters. It is also a time when the candidate can let the voters know what his or her qualifications are and why he or she would make a good leader.

2. Read a portion of John F. Kennedy's speech when the accepted the Democratic presidential nomination in 1960:

   The new Frontier of which I speak is not a set of promises - it is a set of challenges. It sums up not what I intend to offer the American people, but what I intend to ask of them.

3. The assignment is to write a presidential campaign speech for a famous person - past or present. Some examples of the candidates the students might choose are:

   ALEXANDER GRAHAM BELL
   THOMAS EDISON
   BENJAMIN FRANKLIN
   BETSY ROSS
   MARTHA WASHINGTON
   CHRISTOPHER COLUMBUS
   BILL GATES
   WILL SMITH
   HILARY CLINTON
   COLEN POWELL
   BRITTANY SPEARS
   BRAD PITTS
   REV. JESSE JACKSON
   MICHAEL JORDAN

4. When the students have completed the assignment, you can ask for a volunteer to offer to read his or her campaign speech. A variation would be if the student does not announce to the class the name of his or her candidate. The class would have to guess who the candidate is, based on the information in the speech.

**HIGH SCHOOL
ACTIVITY TWENTY**

BLUEPRINT FOR SURVIVAL

1. Divide the class into groups of four or five students each.

2. Set the scene for this activity:

    You and your party are on a small Lear jet, headed for a tropical island resort.
    Somewhere between America and the island, your plane crashes into the ocean.
    The only survivors are you and the members of your group. No one knows you
    are missing because they do not expect to see you for a week. You must decide
    how you will survive until you are rescued — and you know that the rescue is at
    least seven days away.

3. Put the following "Blueprint for Survival" on the board. Students must then devise
their own solutions for each of the situations.

BLUEPRINT FOR SURVIVAL

-   CHOOSE A LEADER
-   DESIGN A SHELTER
-   CREATE A 24 HOUR WATCHMAN SCHEDULE
-   DECIDE HOW YOU WILL GET FOOD
-   DESIGN WEAPONS
-   CREATE A SIGNALING DEVICE
-   DESIGN A RAFT

4. When the students have completed the assignment, ask for volunteers to share their
blueprints with the rest of the class.

APPENDIX

SCHOOL INFORMATION

School: _____

Address: _____

Telephone: _____

Principal(s): _____

Vice Principal(s): _____

Substitute Teacher Coordinator: _____

School Hours: **Begin Day**   **End Day**

      Teachers   _____   _____

      Substitute Teachers   _____   _____

      Students   _____   _____

Dress Code:

      Teachers: _____

      _____

      Students: _____

      _____

School Colors: _____

Parking:

      Teachers: _____Permit Necessary? _____

      Students: _____

School Information
page 2

Fire drill procedures:_____

_____

_____

Tornado drill procedures:_____

_____

_____

Other emergencies (bomb scare, intruder, etc.):_____

_____

_____

<u>Classroom Emergency Situation Procedure</u>

Emergency medical situation:_____

_____

Fight in or outside classroom:_____

_____

Suspected student drug possession:_____

_____

Suspected student weapon possession:_____

_____

_____

School Information
page 3

<u>Location and Telephone Extention Numbers of Important Personnel and Facilities</u>

Principal's office _____ Ext. _____

Vice Principal's office _____ Ext. _____

Substitute teacher coordinator's office _____ Ext. _____

Administration office _____ Ext. _____

Nurse's office _____ Ext. _____

Guidance counselor's office _____ Ext. _____

Resource Officer's office _____ Ext. _____

Teacher's cafeteria _____ Ext. _____

Student's cafeteria _____ Ext. _____

Media (library) _____ Ext. _____

Sign in sheet _____

Mail boxes (incoming) _____

Mailboxes (outgoing) _____

Teacher's rest rooms _____

Student's rest rooms _____

Teacher's planning room _____

Teacher's lounge _____

Teacher's smoking area _____

Snack / vending machines _____

CLASSROOM INFORMATION

Teacher's name _____

Classroom location _____

Subject(s) taught _____

Duty station _____

Location of key(s) _____

Names / locations of neighboring teachers:

_____

_____

Schedule

Period	Time	Subject	Textbook	Class Size

Location of attendance sheets _____

Classroom Information
page 2

Location of seating chart _____

Location of textbooks _____

Location of teacher's edition of textbook _____

Location of various teaching / student supplies _____

_____

_____

Instructions on Operation of Audio / Video and / or Computer Equipment

Television (Note: If there is a school production and if so, times when it is to be viewed)

_____

_____

Video cassette recorder (VCR) _____

_____

_____

Overhead projector _____

_____

_____

Computer _____

_____

SEATING CHART

BOOK APPROVAL FORM

As a substitute teacher, I am expected to have alternate activities on hand to use in the event that lesson plans are not available, or are inadequate for the allotted class time. The following is a list of books that I would like to use in the classroom in conjunction with Literature/Composition activities when I am employed as a substitute teacher at

Name of School _____

Could you please review the list and approve or reject each book on the list? Thank you for your cooperation in this matter.

Signed _____ (Substitute Teacher) Date _____

Signed _____ (Librarian)   Date _____

(AP) Approved for use in the classroom
(NAP) Not approved for use in the classroom

(____)   Book Title   _____

            Author(s)   _____

(____)   Book Title   _____

            Author(s)   _____

(____)   Book Title   _____

            Author(s)   _____

(____)   Book Title   _____

            Author(s)   _____

(____)   Book Title   _____

            Author(s)   _____

NOTES TO THE CLASSROOM TEACHER

Date: _____

Assignment: _____

Substitute Teacher: _____

Absent Students: _____

_____

Tardy Students: _____

_____

Lesson Plan (lesson that students completed): _____

_____

_____

Behavior Problems - Student / Action / Resolution: _____

_____

_____

Special Helpers: _____

_____

_____

Calls, Messages, Visitors: _____

_____

_____

Comments: _____

_____

_____